Cooking *for the* Common Good

Cooking *for the* Common Good

The Birth of a Natural Foods Soup Kitchen

Larry Stettner and Bill Morrison

With Prologue and Epilogue by Sarah Hinckley

North Atlantic Books
Berkeley, California

Published by
North Atlantic Books
P.O. Box 12327
Berkeley, California 94712

Illustrations by Frances McCormick and
   Nancy Diedricksen
Cover and book design by Susan Quasha
Printed in the United States of America

Cooking for the Common Good: The Birth of a Natural Foods Soup Kitchen is sponsored by the Society for the Study of Native Arts and Sciences, a non-profit educational corporation whose goals are to develop an educational and cross-cultural perspective linking various scientific, social, and artistic fields; to nurture a holistic view of arts, sciences, humanities, and healing; and to publish and distribute literature on the relationship of mind, body, and nature.

North Atlantic Books' publications are available through most bookstores. For further information, visit our Web site at www.northatlanticbooks.com or call 800-733-3000.

Library of Congress Cataloging-in-Publication Data

Stettner, Larry, 1938–
 Cooking for the Common Good : the birth of a natural food soup kitchen / Larry Stettner and Bill Morrison.
    p. cm.
 Includes index.
 Summary: "A history of the Common Good Soup Kitchen, a volunteer-run community café and free soup program on Mount Desert Island, Maine"—Provided by publisher.
 ISBN 978-1-55643-957-5
 1. Common Good Soup Kitchen—History. 2. Soup kitchens—Maine—History. 3. Food cooperatives—Maine—History. 4. Natural food restaurant—Maine—History. 5. Soups. 6. Cookery (Natural foods) I. Morrison, Bill (William G.), 1953- II. Title.
 HV696.S6S74 2010
 363.8'83—dc22

                    2010020203

          1 2 3 4 5 6 7 8 9 UNITED 14 13 12 11 10

This book is dedicated to the
spirit of Paul Newman,
whose work inspired the
Common Good Soup Kitchen.

Free Soup Every Week
NOVEMBER THROUGH APRIL
Fearless Optimism in a Bowl

The Common Good Soup Kitchen Community Program will be holding "soup events" and distributing soup weekly all winter, starting the first week in November and going through the end of April. At these soup events a selection of healthful, nutritious soups will be served along with live music or other forms of entertainment, so as to have a place for people in the community to come together on a regular basis during the "quiet" six months. Our volunteers will also be present at these events to pick up soup in containers and deliver it to senior residences and others who cannot get down to the event. Folks who come down to the event in person can also take home soup for themselves, as long as the supply lasts. Our soup events will take place from noon to 2 p.m. on Fridays at our Seawall location—the site of the former Annabelle's Seawall Dining Room at 566 Seawall Road. *Everyone* is welcome at these events, regardless of age or status. The money we have raised this past summer allows us to hold free soup events and deliver soup free of charge all winter. (We do know that some folks feel that they can help and want to; we respect that feeling, and they can always make a donation or volunteer their services, if they so desire.) Frankly, we are hoping to change what people think of when they hear the words "soup kitchen"—the Common Good is a place for fun as well as food; an attractive space for the community to enjoy, for folks to gather, interact, and help each other. There will be vegetarian soups that contain no animal products whatsoever, and meat- or seafood-based soups as well, always using as organically based and locally produced or harvested ingredients as possible. E-mail us at commongoodsoup@gmail.com or call 266-2733 for more information or to inquire about becoming a volunteer for the Common Good. Look for the "Soup Today" sign in the parking area near the road down next to the Seawall Motel every Friday and come on in.

Contents

Acknowledgments

This book as a project was initiated by Richard Grossinger, the publisher of North Atlantic Books, and brought to fruition through the efforts of copyeditor Denise Silva and project editor Erin Wiegand. We owe all of them a great debt of thanks for making the telling of this story possible.

The Common Good Soup Kitchen came to be because volunteers from all walks of life believed in it and contributed their energy to make it happen. These include, but are not necessarily limited to, all those named below. It truly takes a village; we and our entire community are in their debt.

Melanie Anderson

Eli Barlia

Ben Baxter

Allison Bell

Mike Bennett

Lynn Brown

Susan Buell

Evin Carson

Bruce Cassady

Casey Cave

Debra Chalmers

Lynne and Jim Chamberlain

Phil Chipman

Jan Church

Jennie Cline

Gabriella Coniglio

Cassandra Crabtree

Harmony Crossman

Dennis Damon

Emily Davis

Dick Dimond

Muk Dodge

The Dog Mountain Boys

Jordan De Salvo

Laila Dekkaki

Chuck Donnely

Carol Dow

Annie Dundon

Carolyn Dyer

Freya Elizabeth

Robin English

Eleanor Falcichio

Rick Foster

Jill and Bob Freundlich

Matt Gerald

Sheldon Goldthwait

Mark and Jull Kanter

Dr. Geoffrey Knowles

Fay Lawson

Nan Lincoln

Vickie and Dave Lloyd

Gillian Lobkowicz

Marsha and Charlie Lyons

David Mack

Sara MacQuinn

Karin Marchetti

Acknowledgments

Rob Marshall
Fran Martin
Marilyn Mays
Mary McClaud
Gillian Morrison
Dr. Meryl Nass
Alexis Newell
Susan Newman
Antony Nicholson
Leanne Nickon
Zoey Noelle
Mike Odonnel
Leanne Nickon
Heidi and Judah Pelligra
Frank Pendola
Anthony Periale
Teri Peterson
Vivian Phillips
Diane Phipps
Virginia Pierce
Mary Porter
Michael Povich
Sandi Read

Cathy Reed
Louise Rich
Diane and John Ringseizen
Janice and Bunny Roberts
Ruth Roberts
Phil Rogers
Kimmee Ross and Alan Schuman
Ben Rothman
Joni Roths
Ann and Mike Sanders
Mike Sawyer
Geoffrey Schuler
Jeff Shuler
Linda Shultz
Weslea Siddon
Mary Spence
Deborah Stahlman
Gerry Stanley
Alan and Dana Stevenson
James Tarnow
Mary and Jim Vekasi
Arnold and Reva Weisenberg
Hanna Whalen

Prologue
Sarah Hinckley

Inspired by his experiences in his grandfather's restaurant, Bill Morrison began cooking for the Boston public in his early twenties. Enthusiasm and curiosity about the art landed him in some of the more interesting food scenes of Massachusetts's greatest metropolis. After studying under different international chefs for a number of years, Bill gained a reputation and was hired at a chic new bistro. "It was the mid-1980s, back when the United States was thriving on self-indulgence," says Bill with a shake of the head and his best wicked Jack Nicholson smile. At this particular nightclub, patrons were indeed indulged in rich foods laden with dairy. Burgers made with expensive beef were piled high with exotic fixings. Champagne flowed, and food was only one of a slew of vices that enticed the establishment's regulars.

Bill soon burned out on the nightlife. Arriving home from work when the rest of the world was waking up to start another day began to wear on the young chef. When a friend invited him to the Shree Muktanada Ashram run by the Siddha Yoga Foundation in Chestnut Hill, a suburb of Boston, Bill accepted. Within the serene walls, he discovered not only an enthusiasm for a new way of life but also a renewed excitement for food.

The energy at the ashram was exactly what Bill was looking for. As frequenters and authorities of the ashram discovered Bill's talent in the kitchen, they began requesting his cooking skills. Followers of the Gurumayi ate a mostly macrobiotic diet. Already diversely trained in cooking French, Indian, Japanese, and Chinese cuisines, Bill quickly incorporated vegetarian food as a regular part of his repertoire. At the ashram he was trained in preparing nutritious whole foods, and learned to use tofu not in the Western fashion (dressing it up to taste like chicken or serve as a meat substitute) but more in the fashion of Asian cuisine (where it's an integral part of a meal).

Bill's experience at the ashram helped shift his lifestyle from overindulgence at the nightclub to conscious refinement in living and eating, and prepared him for his next job as a chef at the only macrobiotic restaurant in Boston. There, Bill's mentors were leading chefs in the macrobiotic world, and he spent four years at the restaurant. He enjoyed being involved with a group of people who were very intent on food—everyday food.

What made the cuisine new and different for Bill was the emphasis on omitting dairy, while implementing seaweed, select seafood, and whole grains. Featuring vegetables as the main course versus meat was also a key element of the macrobiotic diet. Following this lifestyle, Bill became much thinner and healthier than he had been at any other time in his life. Food was the biggest factor of his improved lifestyle. Though he did not become a vegetarian, he did alter his diet to include a greater percentage of vegetables with rice and beans (as opposed to the largest percentage of one's diet being meat), to maximize on nutrients and maintain a healthier functioning body.

Nearly a quarter of a century later, after being laid off from a restaurant he helped design and open, Bill returned to the principles ingrained during his time at the ashram. There is a photo of Gurumayi hanging on the wall of his kitchen in Southwest Harbor village. Although meditation is not a regular part of Bill's existence, it is something he admits he calls on in times of need. For many artists, meditation can often be accomplished through their medium or method, which may be why Bill decided to keep cooking, even without having a venue to serve the public—yet.

To fend off the doldrums of unemployment, Bill would often take the items in his refrigerator and craft a pot of soup. A number of others in the community who were also between jobs began to gather around the chef and his pot of soup, creating an impromptu soup kitchen: "My house started becoming this place that people came to ... what I was doing with the food was kind of irrelevant."

What began as a way to pass the time soon gained momentum and purpose. Unemployed members of the community showed up to help put together the week's offering. Friends gathered to help make and then partake in the soup. By "doing the soup," those who participated felt useful; they had a sense of purpose. And by distributing it to friends and neighbors they were contributing to the well-being of others in their community.

"They just needed to not be depressed," said Bill, who found tasks for helpers like cutting vegetables and picking herbs. He had taken his skills and experience from back at the ashram and created a place of shelter and community for people who were out of work. The soup kitchen even helped some of them with their job searches: "Once they did the soup, all of a sudden they'd have good luck and they'd get a job. I'm the only one that hasn't," Bill added with a chuckle.

Bill had cooked for the ashram for nearly a decade, in the Boston location and in the Catskills, at times for thousands of people. There was an intent in making the food, in preparing whole foods, natural foods. There was a discipline to the process of gathering the foods and cooking them. Preparing soups in his home kitchen in Maine, that same intent was present, within Bill and within those coming to assist. "They became just choppers. At the ashram there were choppers too, no political discussions, no judgment, just chopping. Eventually it is simply about getting large amounts of food processed and contributing to the greater community." The importance of food in creating and sustaining community had never been clearer to Bill, and this experience helped shape his vision for a community soup kitchen, co-op, and café. In the chapters that follow you'll hear the story of how Bill's vision was realized: in chapters 2–4, 7, 8, 12, and 16 Bill shares his methods, stories, and philosophies of cooking and of the influence of food in his life, and in chapters 1, 5, 6, 9–11, and 13–15, his partner Larry narrates the compelling history of the Common Good Soup Kitchen Community as it was lived through *his* eyes.

1
February:
Just a Walk in the Woods

It was the first of November 2009. Larry sat on a wooden folding chair next to a small metal table in the hallway near the elevator on the second floor of the Harbor House Community Center in Southwest Harbor, Maine. He read over the flyer one more time. He had crafted it carefully to represent all the elements they were trying to get across: that the soup events were free of charge; that no one had to feel pressure to make a donation, but at the same time no one had to feel guilty because donations were always an option; that the events were for everyone in the community; that these were

Sofia, Larry's Spinone Italiano. It was during walks with her that the collaboration began that led to the Common Good.

fun gatherings and not grim line-ups for a bowl of soup; that this would be a consistent program all winter; that the soup delivery program and take-out was continuing; that the soups featured organic, healthful ingredients but were not exclusively vegetarian; and that the operation could use more volunteers. This was a lot to get on one page! Larry was feeling really good—they had done it. Without any outside funding or major donors, without a church or other institutional sponsor, they had amassed enough financial and human resources to be able to put out that flyer with confidence that the program it described was solidly in place.

What's more, he was sitting there on the first Sunday in November, the day when the Westside Pantry food voucher program (which issued vouchers to residents that they could use to make purchases from three local grocery stores) opened for the season. For months Larry and his team had been talking about working in concert with the Westside Pantry, and being present when the vouchers were given out to let those folks know about the Common Good community. Now it was happening, and they were there. He had two volunteers with him and lots of flyers, and they were positioned where people had to pass them on the way out after receiving their vouchers. They were no longer just talking the talk—they were walking the walk.

A sense of what could best be called quiet elation filled Larry's not insubstantial belly space, a very calm yet very deep-down satisfaction that was both relaxing and exhilarating. A feeling not quite like anything he had ever known before. As people began to file in, he reflected on what it had actually taken to get to this point, how he had been slow on the uptake in realizing that it would ultimately require *his* fearless optimism as well as that of a lot of other folks to make the common good program happen ...

It had started one day nine months earlier, when Larry heard his cell phone ring—a good old-fashioned ring-ring-ring sound, just like a real phone. Larry liked it that way. It was Bill Morrison, the chef, who mentioned that he needed some advice and asked to meet with Larry to talk it over. Now, though Larry had known Bill for years, patronized his restaurants, greatly admired his cooking, seen him around town, and even played poker with him, this was only the second time that Bill had ever called him to talk about something. The first time had been that past summer when Bill's teenage daughter was suffering from an unrequited crush on Larry's most handsome teenage grandson, but that was long blown over, so this had to be something else.

Larry liked Bill and enjoyed talking to him, so he was curious and intrigued. They arranged to meet the next day, during Larry's afternoon walk with his dog Sofia in the old wild blueberry field just on the edge of town. Larry's time was kind of tight these days. He devoted his prime effort to his wife Franny, who had memory problems and could function well only with the help that Larry could provide. Then there was all the household stuff to do, the eight-month-old puppy, the weekly music that he booked for the local café with attendant press releases, keeping up with family and friends and planning visits, the little essays about life in Maine that he wrote on a pretty regular basis for his blog group, and so on. All in all, enough to keep an old retired dude pretty busy.

It was a sunny day, mild for February. As the men walked down the abandoned dirt track that bisected the field, the dog romped among the undulating landscape of dormant plants and bushes of a blueberry field in winter. There were boulders strewn around, mini-ravines and crests, a pond and a stream—all remains of the last glacier of the Ice Age.

"I guess you heard I've been laid off," Bill said after a long silence. Bill had been working as a chef at a local café for the last three and a half years, but business had been slow since the economic downturn in the winter of 2009. "But I'm trying to be philosophical about it," he continued. "Maybe it's a sign. Maybe it's time for me to pursue my real dreams."

"Like what?"

"I've had this idea gnawing at me for a while. I've been thinking about starting up a local store or co-op for natural foods, grains, and local seafood. We could really use something like that here. The entire time I was working at the café, I was frustrated that we didn't have access to local food. I mean, we live in a fishing community, but we buy our 'local' fish from Portland or Boston!"

The dirt road led to a small opening in the woods and then a wider hiking trail through a pine and spruce forest. "So that's what I wanted to talk to you about today," Bill explained. "I've seen what you did with the music thing at Sips; you obviously have some organizing skills. Do you have any advice for how I could start up a co-op store like this?"

Larry mentioned that he had been involved in one Mount Desert Island start-up venture, though only peripherally: some locals had founded a senior college, basically an elder hostel program, which offered senior citizens enrichment classes on a regular basis at various locations, and was now an entrenched institution. He explained, "They got going by putting an ad in the local papers and holding a meeting in the Somesville firehouse for interested folks." Somesville was just about in the center of the island, fifteen minutes from Bar Harbor and fifteen minutes from Southwest Harbor. Though there was certainly other work involved, this was all it took to get things rolling: "Enough folks were attracted to that meeting to get the program launched." He suggested that Bill take the same path: "Get a small group of people together first, work out a plan or proposal, advertise it in the papers as a general meeting, and see how many people show up, how much interest it will generate."

They tossed the idea around and discussed the ideal location of the co-op. Larry was pretty familiar with the co-op in Blue Hill, a town across the bay to the west, about an hour's drive from where they stood. It was a place where the '60s lived for Larry and it seemed quite successful. With that as a model, Larry thought a co-op here would have to be central, drawing from the whole island, as the entire year-round population for all the Mount Desert Island (MDI) towns combined was only ten thousand. But Bill was thinking more locally, and had a gut feeling that he wanted the focus to be right in Southwest Harbor.

They paused to let Sofia sniff her way around some particularly tempting bushes, glancing back at the men every so often for approval. Their conversation turned to what Bill called the politics of food: "When I first encountered macrobiotic cuisine back in Boston years ago, it was associated with a restaurant run by a small religious group. One day they looked at me and said, 'What are you doing here? You are not one of us.' I simply replied, 'I am here for the food.'" Bill went on to explain how he had put the knowledge he had acquired to good use in cooking for large numbers at an ashram in the Catskills, the mountains north of New York City where former resorts had been ripe for turning into spiritual retreat centers, and that he hoped to expose even more people to this lifestyle. "Eating nutritiously is something that *everyone* should have access to," he insisted.

The politics of food, as Bill discussed it, was a concept that resonated with Larry, who recognized that food preferences and social strata, subcultural attitudes and beliefs, as well as economic status were intertwined in the United States. He told Bill about a documentary he had seen on public television years ago that had left an indelible impression. It was about the culture conflict that occurred when a small town in western Massachusetts became a haven for high-tech employees moving out from the Boston area; the locals considered it was an invasion of outsiders, and the new residents thought that the locals were stodgy and set in their ways, obstacles to progress. At one point a new coffee shop opened on Main Street. A local spoke to the microphone held by the filmmakers: "Look at the sign in the window. *Cappuccino*," he muttered bitterly. "Whatever happened to just plain old coffee? They might as well say 'locals keep out.'"

"Now Dunkin' Donuts sells cappuccino and it is as American as apple pie," chuckled Bill. "Maybe sushi was the cultural fault line now," Larry thought. But that was changing rapidly. "How long will it be before McDonald's unveils McSushi?" he wondered aloud. As they made their way back toward the parking lot, enjoying the beauty of the crisp afternoon and the rapport of their walk, they mused some more. They both agreed that the real challenge was to get natural food, organic food, healthy nutritious food into the mainstream—not just appeal to the already converted, the folks who went to Bar Harbor or Ellsworth or even all the way to Blue Hill to shop for these foods, but to establish something local, something community-friendly that would attract new people to this kind of food. So the co-op would have to be a warm, inviting place, with affordable food and fun events to draw people in.

"I have no doubt that if you are involved, there will be fun events happening there," said Bill, his eyes twinkling as Sofia gracefully leapt into her back seat in the car and the two rather large men lumbered behind the wheel into each of theirs.

Larry smiled and then drove home thinking that this was an interesting afternoon conversation, and then turning his thoughts to other things. He had no inkling what this afternoon conversation had set in motion, how a gently flowing stream of curiosity eventually would become a roaring river of total obsession.

2
The Soup Manifesto:
A Memoir and History

Soup, I realize now, has been a theme throughout my whole life. As a boy, soup was a warm place surrounded by family, especially since my grandfather owned a diner. As a young chef, it could be artwork—creating soups, stews, and chowders could break the boredom of routine. Today my pursuit is almost bordering on obsession, but I hope it's an obsession with a purpose. And now as I dip into soup history, it occurs to me that soup is also a theme in history—and there is a specifically American version of that history. Basically, if you have fire, a pot, and water to put in the pot, you can have soup. What to put in the simmering water is the question. For that, we need to conjure up the voices of our ancestors. I imagine there was a first pot of soup, but as with Columbus, Edison, and the Wright Brothers, the idea of "the first" is eclipsed by the many pioneers working toward a common end.

The key was the pot, just as it is today. The first watertight and heatproof containers arrived on the cooking scene about five thousand years ago. These containers held the first essential ingredient—boiling water. Boiling expanded the range of foods that our ancestors could consume. It made more use of animal foods, especially bones and tough portions of meat. The simmering water softened hard vegetables and roots that were previously difficult if not impossible to consume. Plus, there was conservation of heat, because hot water imports its energy evenly and at a lower temperature.

The most pivotal thing born of this pot of simmering liquid probably could be called the beginning of cuisine itself, and that is *flavor.* We discovered that one unique taste would rise from a concoction of many ingredients and many flavors. This one taste would import itself into the liquid over time, at last revealing itself to the cook, who could announce, "It is ready ... It is done." The Japanese have a term for this—*umami,* also called "the fifth taste." The translation is something like "delicious flavor," the term for the taste that follows the four essentials—salty, sweet, sour, and bitter. The French use terms like *saveur*—basic essential taste—and in English we have *savory.* With this new taste came another very important element and a new question: does the person tending the pot know what he or she is doing?

We do know that soup has been consumed in the Mediterranean since Neolithic times. Ancient peoples used liquid food for invalids. Medicinal herbs and spices were added to create appetite in people with stomach ailments. Throughout Europe and the Middle East people used these methods to create soups, stews, pottages, gruels, porridges, broths, consommés, etc., all evolving from local tastes. After people settled in the New World, soup naturally evolved into an American staple. Some early colonial cook books contained recipes for soup, and as immigrants from various areas of Europe arrived, they brought their traditions with them. At the beginning of the twentieth century, soup entered the industrial world when a pair of cherub-faced twins claimed that Campbell's Soup was "M'm M'm Good!" Campbell's, one of the most prolific advertisers of all time, developed the first "condensed" canned soup, a method that made its transportation more feasible and economical. One of our most common cultural images of soup is from the 1960s and '70s, when Andy Warhol rendered the Campbell's Tomato Soup can with multiple colors, making a pop art icon out of an industrialized product.

But to me, the image that epitomizes the enduring qualities of soup is from the 1930s: the railcar travelers popularized by Woody Guthrie. I imagine a gathering of men in disheveled, tattered suits sitting around a campfire. On the makeshift fire grate sits a can of soup or beans, lid pried open, like an original feast. In this manner, soup represents a true and organic manifestation of "grace." And today, now that money is once again disappearing and the food supply is being disrupted, the art of soup can return as a saving grace.

My introduction to soup was back in the 1950s at Hennessey's Spa, my grandparents' restaurant in Lynn, Massachusetts. My Irish grandfather, George, opened his working man's–style café with my grandmother in the late 1940s, serving what they called French-American foods. Hennessey's Spa was across the street from St. Mary's Parish and was a favorite hangout for the Catholic students. The word *spa*, I imagine, was because they had a classic soda fountain with a marble counter, serving water and syrups and original ice cream floats. I spent many an afternoon sitting at that counter enjoying my favorite foods: my Polish grandmother's cabbage soup, my grandfather's clam chowder, and the imperial BLT sandwich. I was teased endlessly by my sisters for how often I ordered these items. My grandmother would reassure me that my taste in food was excellent and that my grandfather actually invented the BLT. Papa George would yell from the open kitchen, "Lotte, don't lie to the boy!" and Nana would cover my ears and swear at him in Polish.

Even though my grandmother often overplayed things, with comments like, "Oh, what a party" when the restaurant was empty, she was right about one thing—my grandfather was an excellent cook. I didn't get to spend time with him literally in the kitchen. No one did. He was a madman at the stove. He would run over you if you got in his way, yelling, "Lotte, get your kids out of here before they end up in the soup!" He only took a break to smoke a Pall Mall and then got back at it. Papa George was a true working chef. I learned two basic things from watching him from my perch at the counter: (1) there is a right way to cook, and (2) there is such a thing as good food, and all food is not good food. To this day, I still have not tasted chowder as good as his.

I also learned a lot about cooking from watching my mom at home. She was the only one allowed to cook with my grandfather, and it was inspiring to watch her create magic in her own kitchen. But my mother, bless her, for some reason also embraced the "new" and "modern" foods of the 1950s and '60s—foods like Tang, Ring Dings, Twinkies, Campbell's Tomato Soup, and ingredients like packaged dressing mix, saccharin, and powdered coffee creamer. Having grown up in the Depression, my parents considered these to be almost miracle foods. Like everyone else at the time, they were innocents in the commercial foods game. But none of it did her or us much good. Along with Camel Straights—advertised as healthful in the 1950s—these wonder foods took my mother's health. So in my career as a chef, I have naturally pursued and encouraged the use of whole foods, original methods, and awareness of what the body needs, not just wants—"Food for blood, blood for food."

Still true to my childhood cravings, chowder is one of my favorite foods—yet these days, dairy is an irritant to my system. So I have worked to create alternative recipes that marry popular American tastes with more healthful cooking techniques. Japanese cuisine with its use of seaweed has had a great influence on my cooking. Its emphasis on clean flavors, healthy foods, and fresh seafood is a great match here in the Gulf of Maine. In my research on chowder, I discovered that the native Micmac (Mi'kmaq) and Abenaki (Abnaki) people might have been thinking along the same lines. Acadian cookery began when French settlers started trading with the Micmac tribes in the seventeenth century. And, even though the Brits kicked them out, their cookery remained. One of their more enduring collaborations was clam chowder, originally without dairy. Before the French showed up, the Micmacs used a huge kettle made from a hollowed-out tree trunk. Being a "clam culture," into the wood kettle would go soft-shell clams along with eel, lily roots, wild garlic, burdock, dulse, kelp, and sometimes corn and beans if they could trade for them. And the mixture was cooked by tossing in super-hot rocks. So, New England clam chowder was likely birthed from encounters with French settlers armed with their iron cooking pots, or *chaudieres*. (It certainly wasn't influenced by the English Pilgrims, who originally shunned clams and oysters and fed them to their pigs.) The Micmacs happily adapted to the new iron kettle and put their own stamp on it with a decorative pattern that replicated bark. Later, the French and English introduced salt pork, salt cod, and dairy, and a plethora of chowder varieties was created.

Finally, in this brief study of soup, I would have to say that the people who deserve credit for the extensive renditions of soups, purees, peasant stews, bisques, chowders, and more that we know today in America are the French people, specifically the Parisians. If I were to pinpoint it more specifically, it was the Parisian chefs around the time of the French Revolution. The word "soup" itself is derived from the word *soupe*, which describes the foods such as breads or meats that were used to "sop up" the broth, bouillon, or sauce that was commonly served in the inns of France. Eventually the word *soupe* was used to describe the whole entrée.

The word *restor'ant* was first used in Paris to describe a highly concentrated inexpensive soup (a broth reduction) consumed as a restorative and antidote to exhaustion. In 1765, during Louis XV's reign, a man named Boulanger, a vendor of soup in the Rue Poulies, gave his soups the name of *restor'ants*—or "restoratives." His claim to fame was the sign outside his shop that read, "Boulanger sells magical restoratives." The unique thing about his shop was that it was open to the general public. Before that time, one could only get a meal while staying at an inn (and only at fixed times) or at a *traiteur* where one could only order large portions of meat ahead of time. From these shops, which initially sold only *restor'ants* but soon expanded their menu offerings, the term *restaurant* was derived.

The introduction of the restaurant brought immense progress in the culinary arts. Many chefs began to shine in Paris, serving dishes like salted cod in garlic, sheep's feet in broth, and truffle consommé. During the French Revolution restaurants multiplied, permitting everyone to obtain—according to his purse and appetite—copious and delicious meals. Prior to this, such foods were the preference and prerogative of the very rich. As a result of the French Revolution, many noblemen fled France, and their chefs were among the refugees. While some opened restaurants in Paris, others fled to America. Jean-Anthelme Brillat-Savarin, the original food writer and critic, wisely fled to New York. During his time in America, he traveled to Boston to visit his friend and fellow refugee, Jean Baptiste Gilbert Payplat dis Julien, more commonly known as Jean Baptiste. In 1794, Baptiste opened an establishment called "Restorator," specializing in soups, consommés, purees, and bisques. Bostonians later referred to the tavern as "Julien's Restaurant" and dubbed him Prince of Soups, calling his famous turtle soup the king of all soups.

Thus, the Parisians were at the heart of what we today consider commonplace, and that is the individual's right to walk into a diner or café and get served. Yet in our modern era we find ourselves at another historical culinary impasse. Today access to whole foods, local organic foods, and sustainable fisheries is more important than ever for our well-being. But, because of economic inequities, good whole food is once again hard to get. Like Louis XVI, the gourmand of gourmands, only the wealthy can eat well today. Organic foods are largely available to the wealthiest and most privileged among us. Let us break down the bastions and make natural, whole food—including organically based soups—for everyone. *Vive la Révolution!*

3

Cooking with Your Instincts: Primal Tastes, Feasting with Fire

Primal Tastes

For years when I was a kid every time I went to a lunch spot or diner I would order a BLT (bacon, lettuce, and tomato) sandwich. To say that I liked this sandwich could not begin to describe my obsession: if a restaurant didn't have it I did not want to eat there. Nothing dulled my desire: not repetition, not teas-ing and harassment from my family, not even a bad BLT. Why? Was I stuck in a food rut? Was I nostalgic for my grandfather's diner? For me the BLT experience was transcendent—it brought me somewhere. But where exactly was it that it brought me? Now that I am a chef (and looking back on it this was inevitable), it is time to figure it out and speak up for myself.

It was the flavor, the final flavor, the emerging flavor—the flavor that came from the combination of toasted white bread, crisp bacon, fresh tomato, lettuce, and mayonnaise blended together to make one taste. My body recognized the flavor from the first bite. The flavor was authentic; it came from somewhere to be part of me. There is no nostalgia in taste; there is just taste—in the moment, present, uncompromising—the raw experience of the palate. An authentic reproduction of a classic diner, the presentation on the plate, the time it takes to make it—none of these things matter. Close your eyes and take a bite: it is or it isn't the taste.

Flash forward many years and I have the same experience with miso broth. When I first tasted miso broth I knew nothing about it. Miso broth just rang my bell right away. I felt it on my tongue and all through my body immediately. It was primal. Its depth of taste immediately made me interested in Japanese cuisine. So what is that deep down satisfying taste experience about? It feels like history. But is it?

That first feast: What was it? Where was it? The idea that cooking started somewhere sometime starts to boggle the mind if you really think about it and try to pin it down. My curiosity as a chef after thirty-five years has reached beyond my present understanding. There is so much I don't know, so much I never really thought to ask before. These days, when people call me *chef* it feels somehow like they are accusing me of abject madness. I am driven. I want to know: Who was the first human or human ancestor, Homo sapiens, Homo erectis, or Homo habilis, to stick his or her finger into a warm marrow bone or the flesh of a roasted yam and taste it and think, "This is good. Me like. Me like hot food. Me like fire. Maybe me put scrub grass, root, bone and water in gourd. Cook real slow over burning stump—make more yummy?" Okay, sounds goofy, but there had to be an "aha" moment, right?

There is something inherent, something primal, about the feast, isn't there? Let's turn to the natural world. Sea otters love feasting on mussels. They dive for the mussels, bring them to the surface, and while floating on their backs place the mussels on their chests and crack the shells open with a rock, suck the contents down, and then go back down and dive for more. I am envious of this experience. I must admit that I have done something similar, though, sitting on my couch opening the more difficult pistachios! Chimpanzees love ants on a stick. After stripping the leaves off, they poke a long branch into an ant hole and then lick it like a lollipop. I've seen kids do essentially the same thing with a jar of chocolate sprinkles and a straw. The real difference in our feasting though, from that of the sea otter and our primate ancestors, is that we came on to land and out of the trees and moved from raw food to cooked food. The foods that we could then combine in a broth over a fire make us the most omni of the omnivores.

Feasting with Fire

Although food might be "cured" with salt or something acidic, if food is "cooked" then heat is involved. For heat, you need some kind of fire. There has always been fire as a natural occurrence, but for the ancients to really cook they had to control fire, had to know how much fire to use, how fire could be good for the food. The idea of "cooking with fire" had to be conceived. This idea is what eventually through a long and winding road led us to the solid rock foundation of contemporary cuisine in western civilization: the stocks, broths and consommés of Paris, the methods that we use today. The Parisian chefs at that time drew from their cultural experiences and knowledge, but they also drew from something primal.

So how did this human obsession with cooking and taste start? Flavor, flavor from fire. Maybe it all happened like this: Habilines were our first post-ape, pre-human ancestors who came out of the trees, made stone tools, wielded fire sticks, and strode across the grasslands never to look back. (*Habilines* sounds to me like a Syrian cake made of sesame.) It took these habilines a mere million years or so to transition from the posture they had that adapted them to an arboreal environment to become upright, "clever humans." So there was lots of time in trees watching over the grasslands that they would eventually dominate: hours of watching, sometimes with friends. So maybe this is how it started.

Put yourself in the Homo habilis point of view. Imagine hours of sitting quietly, balanced on an acacia tree limb, up close to the soothing canopy, gazing across the Serengeti. (That's after you have eaten the pods, leaves, and the surprisingly good thorns and cleared a nice perch for yourself.) You see huge migrations of non-carnivore beasts (luckily for us protohumans) constantly flowing across the grasslands. They feast on everything that comes up from the ground: fresh grass, dry grass, herbs, tender shoots and roots. In addition to these large animals there are other critters that are harder to see: beetles, moles, mice, snakes and more are down there, munching away. We a get a front row seat in the naturally fire-resistant acacia for the best drama of all—fire.

The grasslands and plains in front of us providing our panoramic view were and are considered a fire-climax savannah: this is where the grasses, bushes, and the other vegetation encourage fire. They are also uniquely equipped to survive and thrive after a blast of fire. This drama repeats itself like a TV series unfolding in front of you, and, like *The Sopranos*, has some predictable results. Grassland fires move so quickly that some animals will get caught unawares. Depending on the intensity things living (all "natural" of course) will get a bit of roasting. Since the Serengeti is packed with wildlife and roots and tubers, this roasting can produce quite a feast. Simply put, when the fire comes and goes all kinds of good food is left underneath the burnt crust. If you were a watchful and very patient being in the trees who was into scavenging, you could be right on time for optimum feasting: roasted meat—tender and rare in the center. Bones with warm marrow centers would be an especially good find as would earth-roasted tubers and roots with sweet soft flesh inside the blackened skins. Your newly chipped flint hand axe makes cutting away pieces and cracking bones that much easier. Everything is easier because of the fire. Chewing is easier. Filling your stomach is easier. Digesting is easier. Certainly the whole process of eating the fire-produced feast is easier than pounding your meat with a rock to try and make it soft. And the taste! A new taste, new divine flavors!

We can't know how long it took for our ancestors' awareness of fire to go beyond the benefits of scavenging after the fact. Somehow the act of watching from the trees and the memory of good food from the fire started the process. Let's say that maybe while in the joy of another natural BBQ feast, a Chef Emeril–type protohuman picked up a smoldering stick and swirled it around in his exuberance. What he noticed then was that the red part of the stick got redder and hotter as it was swirled through the air. As with the origin of many tools of man, for a time the swirling was an object of amusement and fascination. Eventually maybe a more ambitious and clever Homo habilis specimen would bring one of the fire sticks to the next grassland area to light his own fire and see what it produced. Bam! Now he could make the feast happen, something more convenient than watching and waiting for the next naturally occurring conflagration. It all started with flavor: fire-food-flavor. Apparently it is good to play with fire.

The taste and feel of cooked food made a difference. Even a fruit that was already good and easy to eat and digest became even yummier and easier, and lots of new foods came into the picture. Oh, yes, easier to eat and digest is very important. Even today's staunchest all-vegan vegetarians aren't going to be chomping away on a raw potato. Before cooked food, raw was it. There could well have been a lot of beleaguered and somewhat bellicose pre-historic vegetarians bogged down by long bouts of chewing in place; a very nerve-racking state of affairs eating all this raw food. The lucky "new age" protohumans of the time that gathered around cooked food, especially cooked meat, were a lot more social and a lot happier in general. This all started because of the "yumm factor." This factor is both defined and elusive. Lots of names for this muse—*delicious, scrumptious, appetizing, savory, aromatic, delectable.* What is behind these words is the very thing that makes us human— not just the food but the desire for certain kinds of taste in food. The desire for good-tasting food fueled our evolution. It made our brain grow from generation to generation, favored those with the smarts to learn to control that fire.

There is a reason why people today are intrigued yet befuddled by cuisine. How to make a stock, broth, sauce, custard, stew, casserole, mousse, soup, bread, griddle cake, bisque, pulled-pork barbecue, succotash, hush-puppy, or corn-pone? These were once all original and inspired creations; but now in a country packed with foods we have lost our bearings. Desire has run away from its roots as it has run amok. It is taken hold outside of us. It seems now to be driven and funneled by the Food Network, the latest hot restaurant, or the definitive trendy chef or cook book of the moment; but it is actually buried inside of us. It is buried in our instincts. That is how all that good food stuff happened in the first place—creative instincts. Desire for flavor, the quest for the "yumm factor," is eternal. Connect with your inner cook.

4
A Philosophy of Cooking: Methods versus Recipes

Pretty soon now we are going to get to what you expect from a book about food: how to actually cook some things. Before we start doing that though, we have to have a heart-to-heart talk about recipes. I have always had a problem when people have asked me for recipes. They think I am being devious and deliberately secretive when I am not. I just don't think about recipes the way most people do, exactly so much of this and so much of that, precise measurements and so on—what people are used to finding in most of today's cook books. You will find this out in coming to  the back of the house with me in my subsequent chapters on making stocks, soups and whole grain salads (chapters 7, 8, and 12). I think that method is much more important than recipes. A recipe is simply one person's interpretation of a dish. Once a person understands the methods behind achieving a culinary creation, he or she can decide whether the recipe works or doesn't work. Knowing the methods will help you understand whether it's a good recipe or a bad recipe.

Methods are learned mostly by observing chefs in the actual process of cooking. They know how to treat different kinds of foods, how to slice them, how to braise them, how to grill them, and how to preserve them. They know what effects the different methods have on the finished product: its look, its consistency, and its taste. If you understand the basic method behind things you can produce any number of your own recipes. As long as you understand the basic method of making custard, you can make any kind of custard you want. If you are just using recipes and following them to the letter, you may or may not know the methods behind them and thus may not really understand how they work; thus, you are locked into a limited number of recipes.

I tried to explain this to Larry when he first came around and asked me how I came up with my soups each week. I tried to explain that I just took what people gave me or what was cheap that week or what I stumbled across at the market that looked interesting and used my knowledge to create a soup out of those ingredients. I don't think he got it for a while, but when it clicked for him on one particular day, he became very excited. He asked if I thought I could teach people to do what I do, create out of what was there, rather than go in with a fixed notion of the ingredients needed for this or that recipe.

"Sure," I said, "by having them work in the kitchen with me; I have already done it with some young chefs. It's really more about a philosophy: don't let them get locked into a specific set of recipes or a specific cuisine, let them learn to use methods and techniques from a great variety of sources."

Larry partially incorporated my philosophy into our mission statement when he said that we would train people to cook with what was available in the season, but he didn't quite go far enough. He was still thinking about recipes, like "go find a recipe for what is in season." It took him a while longer to really understand. When we were working on a grant application together much further along in our partnership, he wrote this:

"Our idea is to have a centralized philosophy which teaches cooking methods that promote a *de*-centralized food supply! Our Common Good Kitchen fast food restaurant chefs and food entrepreneurs will be trained not to follow standard recipes as do virtually all chain restaurants today, but will be trained and empowered to understand methods so that they can *create* healthy, affordable fast food from their own local sources, thus changing people's diets while shifting the balance towards local, decentralized, high quality food production."

I thought that was fantastic, and it showed me that now he really understood what I had been trying to say to him. I tried to help him further with an analogy: "It's like theme versus narrative, where recipe is the narrative."

"That's a really cool way to think about it," he said, and the next day he handed me the following:

Theme: boy meets girl, they fall in love, something gets in the way, conflict arises, boy loses girl—will they get back together?

Narrative: Dirk Propellant, a rocket scientist in Huntsville, Alabama, meets Mary Goodworks at a party/fund-raiser for the Good Shepherd soup kitchen that she runs. Mary invites him to help at the soup kitchen in the old downtown section of town behind the hospital. Dirk volunteers and there meets Suzette Crepe, a young volunteer with long shiny black hair and big brown eyes, who totally captivates him. She seems to dig him too, and they date and have great fun, but she always leaves him early and never invites him to her home. Turns out she is caring for her aged father, a southern boy of the old school who is totally dependent on her and somewhat of a jealous tyrant as well, and so she does not know if there is really room in her life for Dirk. When Dirk pushes and tells her that she needs to have a life of her own and has to choose who her number-one man is going to be, she cannot imagine deserting her father and tearfully tells Dirk that she cannot see him anymore. What will happen? (There is no limit to the number of narratives one can construct for this theme.)

I thought this was very cool. In the same way, any chef who knows basic methods, is familiar with many different cuisines, and has learned a creative philosophy can write his or her own story, and create a food line that works for his or her time and place. Enough about boy meets girl—now let's explore how method works for creating soup stories in the kitchen.

Vegan "Cream" of Tomato Soup

Campbell's is the world's best-selling soup; its name is just about synonymous with soup. I think the soup most people think about when Campbell's comes to mind is their Cream of Tomato or simply Tomato soup. For me that is partly because of Andy Warhol, and more importantly, because of Ed Sullivan. Growing up, Sunday night in our house was tomato soup, grilled cheese sandwiches, and *The Ed Sullivan Show*. I guess it was a tradition or maybe Ed sold time to the Campbell Company. Who knows? We were very obedient TV viewers who happily watched Disney shows, *Bonanza*, and Ed while we ate.

Last spring I was delivering soup to our senior apartments in town when I got a special request. A sweet but no-nonsense lady asked me if I could make something "normal" like tomato soup. I understood her right away. Sometimes you want something familiar, you don't want challenges. No matter how strange "normal" really is, you have to have it. She wanted good old Campbell's Cream of Tomato soup, or something like it. For me this was a real challenge, because I had to give them that familiar cream of tomato soup experience in a soup that was totally vegetarian and non-dairy. So I utilized a vegan, non-dairy cream base that I had used before for a mushroom soup (see below). I took that base and pureed it into a sauté of the following ingredients. They are listed in the fourfold table format that I will always use for presenting the ingredients of soups and stocks.

core ingredients	spices
additional vegetables	herbs

The core of the dish is always in the upper left, the auxiliary vegetables or other foods are in the lower left, the spices are in the upper right and the herbs in the lower right. This represents the categorical structure of the dish more clearly, and also encourages creativity by allowing one to see more easily where and how substitutions, additions, or subtractions may be made.

CORE INGREDIENTS	SPICES
plum tomato (crushed organic from can)	paprika
olive oil	turmeric (small pinch)
tomato paste	
a little red wine or vegetable stock	

ADDITIONAL VEGETABLES	HERBS
carrot	basil
onion	oregano
garlic	

The lady loved it; it had that familiar taste to her, she did not know that she was eating something different and healthier than the original.

Vegan Cream Base

Peel and rough chop the following vegetables, listed here in order of their percentage in the mix from most to least:

potato	onion
parsnip	garlic
celery root	butternut squash, just enough to give it a butter look
celery	

Braise all of the above together with the following:

olive oil	nutmeg
thyme	coriander
marjoram	black pepper and white pepper

Braise until soft (adding a little vegetable stock as you braise so that you don't brown the base). Add more vegetable stock—enough to get a final consistency of heavy cream; puree it with white sweet miso and sea salt to taste.

In addition to cream of tomato soup, this can be used for cream of mushroom, cream of leek, cream of spinach, cream of garlic and more. Your imagination is the only limit.

Vegan Split Pea Soup with Sassafras

Another traditional favorite for the folks at the senior residence, and a favorite soup of mine as well, is good old New England split pea soup with ham. This too needed a vegan update. The macrobiotic crew I worked with in Boston had a great split pea soup with vegetables like carrot, celery, parsnips, and daikon radish, which is actually sweet when braised. I added herbs like tarragon and marjoram to their version, always looking for the sweetness and spice that you get from the ham. Remember, taste is primal. I started with an image of the taste I wanted to create; I wasn't trying to find imitation ham, I was trying to find something that would put the same taste into the final split pea soup that ham did. Finally, last winter I found it—sassafras.

CORE INGREDIENTS	SPICES
split peas	sassafras root
3 gallons spring water	coriander
white miso	allspice
	nutmeg
	black and white pepper

ADDITIONAL VEGETABLES	HERBS
carrot	sage
onion	thyme
butternut squash	tarragon
parsnip	parsley
celery	
yellow turnip	
wakame *(optional)*	

Take just a *little* sassafras root because it is strong, about a teaspoon of the powdered form or a tablespoon of root chips for 3 gallons of soup. Sauté it with the split peas and onions before you add your original water to cook the split peas. The flavor will penetrate the soup and you won't miss the ham. In fact, one of the ladies down at the senior apartments wanted to know where I had gotten the great ham for the split pea soup. I laughed and told her it was a chef's trade secret.

So, you start with that focus on taste and you know some basic methods and know how to treat your ingredients and some of the tastes they produce individually and in combination; you keep finding out more as you go along, keep experimenting and tasting. Then you just get in the kitchen and get out the knives and the boards and the bowls and turn on the stove and start writing your own stories!

5
March:
The Pot Simmers

Soon after that fateful conversation in the woods, Bill started making soup in his kitchen and distributing it for free to the senior residence in town, the Ridge Apartments. He was assisted by his ex-wife Mary McClaud, who helped with the soup project by accepting donations at her business, the Sargasso Hair Salon. Larry walked into the little storefront salon and was directed to a small round table

Mary McClaud. It was at her Sargasso hair salon that donations for the soup kitchen were first collected.

at the back that held a small, maybe 6 x 9, lined notebook with a soft dark-blue cover. In a neat hand the following was written:

> The soup kitchen is a community service: "Food for the Soul, Fearless Optimism in a Bowl."
>
> 1. We will use natural whole foods; as many as possible being organic.
> 2. The type of soups we make will be mostly whole grains, beans, and vegetables, with no animal products and low sodium.
> 3. We will be happy to receive raw-food contributions for the soup as well as funds.
> 4. The idea is to provide healthy soup to anybody that needs or wants it at no cost to them.

> The model we would like to use is that of the soup kitchen
> of the 1930s. That is: *No Politics, No Bull, Just Soup.*

Larry was impressed with the simple eloquence, the degree to which Bill had thought this out, and the playful spirit that the appeal seemed to radiate. There were some greenbacks tucked into the middle of the book, maybe fifty dollars worth, and Larry added a twenty.

Later that day Larry popped over to the source of the soup, Bill's home kitchen. It was one short block down and one block over from the hair salon, literally around the corner. Larry climbed the stairs at the side of the house and crossed a small deck that opened right into the kitchen. There were pots simmering and bowls of neatly sliced and diced veggies all over the place; soup was being created. Bill was cheerful and energetic, and excitedly told Larry how the thing had started.

"Mary and I were discussing the fact that it was hard times in Southwest Harbor, a cold winter and an economically bleak one for a lot of folks. She suggested that I could do something for the community, that I could make a community supper to lift people's spirits. That night around 3 a.m. I thought, hey, a supper would be just a one-time thing, so why not make soup for people every week?

"When I was walking downtown the next day I bumped into Barbara Campbell from the Westside Pantry, and she told me I could bring the soup to the Ridge Apartments, the senior residence complex in town. They could use some better nutrition, something special to look forward to each week, some fearless optimism of their own."

And so it began for Bill: early in the week he planned what to make based on what people donated, how much money he had available, whether he could get a ride up to Bangor to the local whole-food grocery or whether he had to shop locally. Bill decided to make vegan soups because that way it was simpler to keep them healthful—low fat and low sodium—plus soups with no animal products keep longer and the ingredients are less expensive. This way he got more nutritional and shelf life bang for a buck. He put his own money into the purchases if donations did not cover expenses that week.

He began chopping and peeling and dicing and slicing Tuesday night or Wednesday, cooking things on Thursday, packaging in containers on Friday and then delivering Friday afternoon, hanging out with the seniors who were in the lobby when he arrived with the soup. Word started to get around. People asked if they could buy soup and he said no, it was not for sale, but anyone could come to his kitchen and get soup when it was ready on Thursdays or Fridays, and contributions were welcome. Some folks came by and picked up soup for other folks who could use it but couldn't get out easily.

"I was worried about what my landlord would think," said Bill, "but then he walked in one time when I wasn't home and left a hundred-dollar bill on the table with a note saying, keep up the good work."

Bill was beginning to feel that he had started something—he was not sure exactly what, but it had some momentum of its own, and it certainly was keeping him occupied for now. Larry was intrigued, enthused even, by what Bill was doing with the soup thing, and he thought it would be good to contribute to it, maybe even attempt to facilitate the effort a bit. He did not yet think of himself as a partner or a co-conspirator; that was still to come.

Bill and Larry got to where they talked on the phone most every day, Bill sharing updates on the progress of the grassroots soup kitchen program. Bill had enlisted some folks to help with the prep—all the chopping and peeling—since it was taking him until three in the morning sometimes to get everything ready for the weekly soup delivery, and he did not want to let down the people at the Ridge Apartments. He was producing in the neighborhood of 50 quarts of soup a week!

Larry looked forward to chewing over (slurping over?) the soup news with Bill, and they scheduled another walk and talk in the blueberry field with Sofia. Bill started off quickly this time and in a serious vein: "What do you think people in this town think of me? Will people really support me?" Larry guessed that Bill's concern about his reputation partly stemmed from his intensity in the kitchen, Bill being keyed up about food production in the heat of the moment as it were in the kitchen; some people could handle this intensity and some could not.

Another factor that he knew weighed on Bill heavily was the demise of his own restaurant six years or so earlier; it was incredibly popular but had been brought down when the new owner of the building decided in essence to evict Bill and put it up for sale; this understandably had left Bill shaken pretty badly.

In reply to Bill's question, Larry said that in a town of two thousand people, there were probably two thousand different Bill Morrisons. "Let me tell you a story," Larry continued, "a story about my John Dorsey. Dr. John Dorsey was a psychiatrist I knew—he had actually spent a year in Vienna as a training analyst with Sigmund Freud himself in the 1930s. He took seriously the notion that one could only know the world through one's own senses, could never know the contents of another person's mind or thoughts, could never know they really existed except as filtered through one's own perception. Thus there was his wife's John Dorsey, not quite the same as his son's John Dorsey, or his neighbor's John Dorsey, etc. There was no *one* John Dorsey. His image of himself was just another image too, hence he never said 'I' or 'me'; he referred to himself as 'my John Dorsey.' An extreme position perhaps," Larry conceded with a smile, "but it is certainly valuable in reminding you of how different people's perspectives can be, of the illusion of finding a unitary 'truth' about any given person."

Larry concluded that *his* Bill Morrison was an okay guy with favorable approval ratings, and that they would just hope that there were enough others in the same ballpark to support Bill's next project. Bill better just accept the fact that there were going to be a lot of different Bill Morrisons out there among the townsfolk, some Bills who wore halos and some who carried pitchforks.

Now they were deep in the woods, past the old gnarled pine tree and on the way down a steep slope to the stream embankment that was the turnaround point. They discussed various aspects of the soup kitchen: the enthusiastic response of the senior citizens, the word-of-mouth interest developing, how good Bill felt to be cooking every week, and how one of the local restaurants was donating their leftover veggies to him each week that he could use as a base for the soups being created.

"This is fun," Bill said, "and gratifying, but I still want to get back to that other thing—figure out how to start the natural food storehouse, the co-op."

Larry thought for a moment, and then he saw it for the first time: "I think you already have," he said.

Bill stopped, also thought for a moment, then he smiled a broad smile and said, "Ya know, I think you may be right, Kemo Sabe!"

Now Larry and Bill really started feeding off each other's energy. Larry noted that a co-op with a built-in a soup kitchen would be unique. Once a week it would provide free soup to all comers; they could do that in a small town, and not fear being swamped as they would in New York or Boston. Bill observed that sharing soup would make the enterprise in effect a community center, providing a place to come together, especially in the winter when people were isolated and times were tough.

Larry started getting really carried away, telling Bill about the drugstore in Wall, South Dakota, that started off years and years ago advertising free ice water with signs on the highway while you were still very far from it. People would stop just to take a look-see and get their free cold lubrication, and now the whole town was a mini-Disneyland, a destination stop. He imagined free soup at the co-op having the same effect, it becoming a major tourist attraction as hundreds lined up for their serving. The two laughed at this, and then Bill said he would start writing up ideas and stuff, making some plans for the co-op that incorporated a soup kitchen.

Over the next ten days or so, Bill had something new to show Larry every day, notes and ideas handwritten on his ubiquitous yellow pads. He brainstormed having all the food in the co-op in the front, on display in bins or barrels or pallets. He noted all the local organic farmers and fishermen that he knew, and how this could be an outlet for them. He wrote about having a seafood co-op within the co-op, about helping to create a market for seaweed and other plants harvested from the Gulf of Maine. Bill shared thoughts about how families in the winter with guys out of work or minimally employed hit a dead spot on Sunday afternoon, and the co-op could be a place to come and bring the kids for a meal and some cheer.

Larry resonated with all this and loved Bill's ideas. He ruminated about how best to organize Bill's spoken and written thoughts into a coherent plan. He chuckled and began to think of himself as James Boswell, recording the utterances of the great Dr. Samuel Johnson. It certainly tickled him to think this, and there was a definite delight and excitement in this sharing of ideas and spinning of dreams, having a "partner in crime," a buddy to work on a project with. He soon changed his imagery and began thinking of themselves no longer as a great man and his doting scribe, but as some kind of dynamic duo like Batman and Robin or, better yet, the Lone Ranger and Tonto (Larry kind of liked being Tonto). He actually went on the Web to find out what *Kemo Sabe* meant; there was some debate, but *faithful friend* seemed to be the consensus.

One lazy morning, as Larry and his wife Franny slept in at their Portland hotel (before catching an afternoon plane to New York for another adventure), Larry received an excited phone call from Bill. "I just picked up this fantastic book, *In Pursuit of the Common Good*, about how Paul Newman's whole salad dressing business got started and it turned into a philanthropic thing. It's a great story—it's very funny and it's everything we stand for. It's inspiring, man, you *have* to read it!"

Larry navigated on foot to the mall near the hotel and wove his way to the Borders bookstore in there somewhere. The book was shelved in the business section, interestingly enough. Larry actually had time to read it over the next ten days during his travels. He too was inspired. Two things stood out to him about the book that he vowed to try to emulate. One, Newman was resolute. He started with an idea—put fresh ingredients in bottled salad dressing—and when people told him he couldn't do it, it wouldn't sell, he did not back off. His attitude was: it can be done if you believe in it and have the will to do it. Second, he maintained his sense of humor about things the whole time, having old lawn-chair furniture in the office, creating silly lyrics to Broadway tunes for his press conferences, making up wild stories for the bottle labels, and so forth. When Larry got back to Maine he suggested to Bill a name for their project: the Common Good Co-op and Soup Kitchen. Bill liked it.

By this time the soup kitchen had morphed into a soup and salad kitchen, now with a name and a significant bit of local buzz. In fact, the local press expressed an interest in running a story, but Bill put them off, wanting to have more of a plan to present before any story ran. He imagined being overrun by hordes of soup-seekers. They started playing around with the idea of having an informational meeting as a possible launch for the co-op/soup kitchen. But before that happened, they hit the first of many bumps in the road.

Larry called Bill one morning and could hear in his voice that he was down. By then it was mid-April, and the weight of the upcoming Maine tourist season was upon Bill in terms of hustling to find a job. In addition, interest in the soup kitchen had waned down at the hair salon—donations were down and the cupboard nearly bare. Larry could hear that Bill was mired in molasses, and needed a boost: not talk, but action. So he told Bill, "Okay, I am coming over. We can talk while I do a small errand, so get ready to go out."

Larry picked Bill up and drove over to the local bank, where they set up a joint account for the soup kitchen, to which Larry made a contribution of a hundred dollars to start it off. Now the soup kitchen had some visible evidence of existence as an entity beyond Bill's kitchen. Just taking this action pulled Bill out of the molasses and he began to plan that week's soup and to put a resume together for a job search.

Larry was reminded of something a very wise psychologist, Silvan Tomkins, said years ago. They were watching a videotape together about a man who had suffered from a long bout of depression. He was telling the interviewer that he finally got fed up with the various drugs and other treatments that had been prescribed for him and decided on some program of his own to cure his depression, which ultimately worked. Silvan had turned to Larry and said, "He doesn't realize that it wasn't the program *per se* that cured his depression—he began to cure it the moment he decided to take action."

6
April:
Digging a Foundation

Project Soup was operating on a weekly basis, and now that Project Co-op was back on the table for active discussion, Larry and Bill were planning a dinner meeting with potential supporters. For inspiration, the two took a trip to Blue Hill, a town across the bay with a successful co-op. Larry always liked visiting the co-op, because it was a trip back in time to the '60s and '70s, for one thing. It was also a thriving enterprise central to town life, well stocked with grains and organic veggies, soy milk

Hannah Whalen. She defined the identity of the Common Good as an innovative program for mind, body, and spirit, and thus launched its mission statement.

and tofu, natural soaps and other oils, and local pottery. It had a small café in the back and volunteer cashiers with tie-dyed T-shirts and long hair and such.

Larry made contact via phone and e-mail and learned about two people whom they should meet with: Hadley Friedman, an employee of the co-op who had recently started a soup kitchen in Blue Hill called the Simmering Pot, and Karen Doherty, the manager of the Blue Hill Co-op who used to live near Southwest Harbor and had even tried to start a co-op on MDI years ago. She would be happy to meet with them. Larry exchanged a few e-mails with Hadley too, and they figured out a way to meet by making a trip to his Blue Hill kitchen on soup day. Based on the e-mail exchanges alone, Larry had formed an image of Hadley in his mind as a lean, somewhat intense, thirty-something guy.

The excursion to Blue Hill took place soon afterwards. When Bill, Larry, and Franny arrived at the church where the Simmering Pot soup days were held, they were a tad late. Bill went inside and Larry parked the car. When Larry came in he saw a guy who seemed to be in charge and who smiled at him, so Larry asked if he was indeed Hadley.

"No," the fellow replied affably, "Hadley is over there." Larry turned and saw an attractive bright-eyed young woman with big brown eyes and jet-black hair engaged in earnest, animated conversation with Bill. He had to reset his image and also reset his internal clock, because he could tell that Bill would be there talking for quite a while.

Larry went back to the car to check on Franny, and found her dispirited at the wait and eager to return home, so it became time for some creative problem solving on a purely personal level. He called a local taxi service, told Bill the new plan, left the car there for Bill (who now could take all the time in the world) and took the cab ride home with Franny. She was still dispirited at first, but the cab driver's continuing folksy down east conversation finally engaged her and changed her mood completely and it was all smiles all around by the time they got back to Southwest Harbor.

That night, Bill reported that Hadley was very dedicated and trying her best to serve healthy and local food as well, and she ran the soup kitchen twice a month and was hoping to expand with the help of another local charitable organization. The meeting with Karen also went well—she was very pleasant and thought that they were "gutsy" because they were just going for it, whereas when she had wanted to start a co-op on the island years ago, she'd spent six months discussing and debating things until it just dissolved. Karen generously sent Larry the Blue Hill Co-op's bylaws, and said she would be happy to help in any way that she could, though her present job was keeping her pretty busy.

Back in Southwest Harbor, Bill and Larry planned some informal dinner meetings to share their plan with the community. Bill whipped up some finger food that everyone enjoyed, as well as soup. At the first meeting people applauded the idea but nothing dramatic happened. At the second, an "aha" moment happened that changed everything. There were seven or eight people involved in the discussion, nibbling on finger food and slurping down soup, when one woman stopped everything by exclaiming: "This is delicious, what *is* this?" Everyone concurred; in fact, it was some kind of wrap Bill had conjured up with cabbage leaf and simple veggie ingredients and spices. So simple, so healthful and nutritious, so scrumptious! Bill and Larry looked at each other. They both saw it at the same moment. This was the way to break through: *prepared*, affordable, delicious, healthy natural food.

The ideas poured out now: they would turn the usual co-op model on its ear and play upon their inherent and unique strength: Bill's incredible talent as a chef. Larry pontificated, first to Bill, then to anyone else who would listen: "Most co-ops start as buying clubs, progress to markets, and then as an afterthought add a little café perhaps, staffed by anyone that they can get. The food is at best okay, the café is really just a place to hang out, fill one's belly a bit along with your herbal tea. The Common Good would turn that around: it would start with a café preparing yummy natural food to attract people, and show what was possible. We would sell the raw ingredients for the food we produce, along with recipe tips and cooking demonstrations, and gradually expand the market/ grocery part of the operation. And, of course we would hold community events, especially in the winter when they are really needed."

Further, with the yummy prepared food and Bill's reputation as a chef, they could really generate some good income from the café part of the business to support the whole co-op operation. Larry had a plan he could sink his teeth into now. He could see it—it was all one big organic whole. The café would sell the healthy prepared food that people could eat in or take out, they would have the bins with the raw ingredients and recipes and talks on nutrition and cooking demos, and people would come and hang out there and slurp the soup and eat the food and drink coffee and talk about stuff, so it would be building community at the same time.

They would serve free soup periodically as well as continue and expand the soup delivery program right out of the same kitchen. The café and takeout business would make money, especially in the summer (when seasonal residents with disposable income or wealth were in town), and this would give them a cushion to operate in the winter. Larry realized with excitement that the transfer of resources from summer to winter was the key to the whole thing. "We *can* make this work in Southwest Harbor," he exclaimed aloud both to Bill and for his own benefit. "The small winter population will not really have to support the enterprise." They would be using and encouraging the production of local food products and seafood and they would create some year-round jobs. One big organic whole, where each of these elements reinforced and stimulated the other.

Bill and Larry took another walk together in the blueberry field with Sofia. Buds were now appearing on the blueberry plants, swollen with the petals that would eventually unfold in May. First delicate pink petals for a short time, and then the longer lasting white ones that would eventually give way to the ripe fruit itself. Bill talked of his cooking innovations and philosophies, and Larry began to see the whole nature of what Bill did as a chef in a new light: he didn't follow some vast library of great recipes in his head. Instead he used food and herbs and spices like an artist would use pigments; he knew them so well that he could put them together to obtain any desired culinary result. He was a true artist, a Picasso who painted with the basic elements of food to produce beautiful cuisine. Larry was inspired in a new way.

Larry wanted to write up a description of this program, what they were then calling the Common Good Co-op and Soup Kitchen, but he was stuck because every time he thought about writing it up he got hung up on the words. It was a co-op but not a traditional co-op, because the emphasis would be on prepared food first and a market second; it was a soup kitchen but not a traditional soup kitchen; it certainly was not a traditional café nor what most people would think of as a community service center. It was all of these but not exactly any one of these as people would think of it. Larry knew that image was important, and that the words "co-op" or "soup kitchen" would create a certain image in people's minds, with emotional connotations and certain expectations; it was hard to think of writing a description where every other sentence would have to be, "but not a co-op the way you think of it," or "not a soup kitchen in the traditional sense."

Larry finally broke out of his block with the help of Hannah Whalen, a professional fund-raiser who had attended one of their early dinner meetings. She had been listening to Larry and Bill, and reading over the awkward one-page summary proposal that Larry had prepared, when she looked up with an air of quiet authority and admiration and said, "You have a very innovative program." Bill just smiled, but Larry responded as if hit by a thunderbolt. "Yes!" he thought, "we are not a soup kitchen, we are not a co-op, we are not a café—we are an *innovative program* with these different yet synergistic elements." At last Larry was unblocked and unbridled, and the pamphleteer of the Common Good had been given a full head of steam. He went home and produced a one-page summary statement of the program that he was happy with, and continued writing in a white heat, producing a mission statement and action plan: nine single-spaced pages incorporating all that he and Bill had discussed and dreamed about. It became their focus, their touchstone, and their primary means for building support for the organization. It also shaped and mobilized their strategy for getting started quickly.

"Maybe we should wait till after the public meeting to share a mission statement," Bill suggested.

"No, we need to have the mission statement already there, have a blueprint for where we want to go and see how many people want to join us."

Larry created the bus trip analogy, the first of maybe a hundred times he would use this analogy that spring and summer. Where would they have been without it? He explained it this way: "Suppose we had an idea for a bus trip, say an excursion from Southwest Harbor to the west coast in the winter of 2010. So we call a meeting to discuss the bus trip, see how many people want to join in. Lots of people show up at the meeting interested in such a trip, but there is still a lot to be determined. Some of the people want to go to San Diego, some to San Francisco, some to Seattle. Some want to leave in early January and some in late March. Then there is the question of what kind of bus, how long the excursion should be, and so on. Committees would have to be formed, votes taken perhaps, to figure out what this bus trip would entail. By the time they decided all this, who knows how long it would have taken or how much enthusiasm would be left for the trip?" Larry and Bill would have a different strategy: they would outline the bus trip in much more detail: it was leaving in early January and Seattle was the destination and it would last three weeks round trip and they were renting a blue bird bus from the Cyr Bus company. This is what they would announce and then see how many people wanted to join *that* trip, how many people wanted to get on their bus. If you wanted to go to San Diego or leave in March then this bus was simply not for you; you would have to make a plan for a different bus trip! Now once folks signed on to the Larry and Bill Common Good bus trip, there were still decisions to be made and they were flexible as to input—there were various routes that could be taken, maybe even detours along the way. The passengers would have their voices heard, but at least every one on the bus agreed on the basics of the destination and the length of the trip! This was the way to move forward.

This is how the mission statement and action plan began:

The Common Good Co-op and Soup Kitchen Mission
- Continue to distribute free soups and whole food salads to senior residences and others in need, expanding to service more people as resources grow.
- Provide local space to store and distribute raw whole grains and natural foods to local businesses and individuals.
- Promote the use of local foods harvested from the sea as well as local produce.

- Educate to teach easy preparation of whole foods and to promote dietary habits which foster health and wellness.
- Help to provide jobs all year round.
- Build and maintain a sense of community year round through sponsoring community events and establishing an inviting space where local residents can always "meet, eat, and greet."
- Provide an avenue for seasonal residents to be involved in supporting the community they love by helping it thrive year round.
- Provide a model of green, eco-friendly living.
- Provide affordable natural food through keeping our costs down and via discounts to Common Good club members.
- Help other local charities and service organizations.
- Produce healthy, delicious soup and whole food salads for sale to support our programs.
- Operate a self-serve café whose revenues will support our programs, and that utilizes the skills of our master chef in preparing delicious natural food.

The statement then went on to give a brief history of how the program had developed out of Bill's soup kitchen, more information on the various elements under each of the points made in the opening list above, and a detailed action plan—which from that point on pretty much took over Larry's life, and ultimately occupied the time and energy of a lot of other folks as well. For Larry, one of the most important sections was where he tried to convey the organic nature, the wholeness, of the proposed program as he saw it:

> Although the above goals are listed separately, the activities of the co-op will typically meet several goals at the same time and will act to augment one another. When a co-op customer comes into the café area and watches our chef prepare soup or salad from the available grains, and then sits down and eats with other customers and finds the food delicious

and satisfying, that person is already sharing an experience with someone else in the community. They are also starting to consume healthier, more nutritiously satisfying food. They are learning by observation how to prepare tasty and satisfying food from whole grains. They are deriving the economic benefit of an inexpensive meal. They are exposed by example to a more economically and ecologically sound approach to meal preparation: using satisfying food that is readily available and affordable rather than having a pre-set idea of what food one "needs" at a given time of the year, even if it has to come from Chile. All of these elements will have been put into play at the same time, synergistically.

In the Back of the House: Preparing Stocks

Chefs that work in restaurants talk about the front of the house and the back of the house. The front is the public area, where the customers sit and the waiters serve them, and any other areas that the public can see. The back is the kitchen area where the chefs do the real work; even in a so-called open kitchen there is usually a private back area where the chefs work out their techniques. In this and my next two chapters I will take you to the back of the house with me.

Paris: City of Lights and Fire Pots

No food method personifies the spirit and taste of the original cooks more than the preparation of stocks, broths, stews, and sauces. The bedrock of all cuisine, the link between the ancient and the present, lies in the method of making stocks, what the late-eighteenth-century Parisians called *restor'ants*. Beef bones, bone marrow, poultry carcasses, root vegetables, aromatic vegetables, and bouquets of herbs—all were components of those ancient fire-produced feasts. What is rendered in the broth, reduction, or sauce is what might be called the *primal flavor*. No group has done more to establish the methods to produce and preserve these ancient tastes that stem from the earth than the original chefs of Paris. Let's pay homage to them, and consider where all of this came from, before we go to the back of the house and get out the pots and knives and start cooking.

In the seventeenth, eighteenth, and nineteenth centuries the preparation of soups, potages, and stocks was a common daily ritual in castles, homes, cabins, and eventually chuck wagons all across Europe and America. Soups were the lifeblood of the home kitchen and required constant vigilance and know-how. If you wanted a warm bowl of soup you had to be home to eat it, and someone had to labor at it; and unless you were wealthy or an aristocrat that person was you or a family member—perhaps someone lower on the pecking order and/or more skilled at tending the pot than you.

Parisians were not the first to make good stocks; they were the first to set standards for stocks, to define what was optimum or ideal. The evolution of methods for making stocks went hand in hand with the development of cooking vessels. A good stockpot is the cornerstone of every chef's kitchen. The Aedui tribe, the original people of Gaul (France), invented metal plating by applying tin to copper and thereby greatly advancing the quality of cooking pots. The metal *chaudron*, or cauldron, thus came into being. Later, probably sometime in the 1600s, the French came up with the first pot that was specific to the making of stock—the *marmite*. The broth that came from this large stockpot was called *petite marmite*. The *marmite* can hold anywhere from five to fifty gallons. The largest ones have a spigot at the base to siphon off the savory elixir that is produced within its confines.

The best by-product of the French Revolution was probably the restaurant. Anybody of any rank could walk into a shop in Paris and get a *soupe*, potage, or consommé. Other establishments specialized in the first rendition of hot chocolate. "Let them eat cake" takes on new meaning in this context: French cuisine for all. Talk about your reversal of fortune! This version of liberty, public access to chef-prepared food, is a cornerstone of our modern culture. We cannot imagine our world without it.

In the Back of the House: Preparing Stocks

After M. Boulanger opened what is considered to be the first Parisian soup shop (or *restor'ant*) in 1765, soup shops very quickly multiplied; it became a collective movement—a mass consciousness like the revolution boiling around him and the other chefs. As the national passion for cutting off heads developed, a similar cleavage through veal bones and such was being carried out all over Paris. There were unemployed homeless chefs everywhere: the chefs from the French provinces had left the comfortable estates of their doomed bosses, hit the road, and all roads led to Paris. Others besides Boulanger expressed their love of liberty through their cuisine. The freedom to use one's talent and create one's own dish or *plats du jour* is the mark of a good chef in today's restaurant world. Before the Paris movement these chefs had to follow the recipes and create the dishes desired by whatever aristocrat they worked for or else. Now in their own shops they exploded like fireworks into brilliant bursts of culinary creativity. They worked at places like *Cadran Bleu*, which stayed open during the storming of the Bastille, and *Café de Roy*, where revolutionaries were actually eating on that fateful day, having a snack for sustenance before they joined in the storming. A bit later, just after the final collapse of the monarchy, three brothers opened the aptly named *Au Trois Frères;* it soon became a mecca for those who wanted to learn the new methods, and became known as the nursery of chefs.

Today's chefs don't make the variety of stocks that were around at the birth of cuisine; even beef and lamb stock are relatively rare now. Chefs like James Beard, Julia Child, Madeleine Kamman, and Jasper White ultimately gravitated to the Cadillac of stock: veal stock. It has the golden color and gelatin content for a particularly good reduction sauce and a rich yet somewhat light and subtle flavor. "Elegantly flavored" stocks are important to competitive chefs and restaurants. I happen to be among those people who are not "down" with veal, though, and veal bones are an expensive specialty item in any case. For me, a poultry skeleton or whole poultry is the best choice for a meat-based stock.

Okay, we're ready now. Come with me to the back of the house; let's get into the kitchen. All those French chefs might be looking over our shoulders but we will just forge ahead; we won't be intimidated. Whatever you put in the pot, most chefs would agree on some universal principles:

- Good stock is essential to cooking savory warm foods, soups, sautés and sauces.
- Use spring water whenever you can; the pure water will do a better job of carrying out the flavor of the stock.
- Use aromatic vegetables, such as carrots, parsley, celery, leeks, and carrot tops.
- Put "earth" ingredients into your soup, like onion, garlic, ginger, etc.
- Caramelize meat and bones. Roast in oven and then brown in a pan; you get more flavor that way.
- Use bouquet garni: incorporate a handful of fresh herbs such as parsley, thyme, marjoram, and so on.
- Go low and slow on the heat, never boil.
- Skim stock while cooking. Debris will rise after vegetables and bone render their juices into the elixir; skim it off and dispose of it.
- Strain and strain again. The finer the sieve, the finer the resulting liquid.
- Cool down before refrigerating.
- Stock will keep in the refrigerator for a week, or longer if it is boiled every four days.

My Methods for Making Stocks: Probably a Lot Like Yours

I use an 18-quart heavy gauge stainless steel stockpot. Heavy gauge is superior for slow cooking. I usually put the pot on the "back burner": remember that low heat, slow and long, renders the best broth. You can get away with 2 hours of simmering for a light stock; it takes longer for a deep brown broth to emerge. Lobster shells definitely take over 3 hours before they give up their entire flavor. There are two ingredients I always use: carrots and celery, the rock stars of the stock world. I use a lot of garlic and ginger. When it comes to onions I like variety—leeks, Vidalias, scallion bulbs, shallots. I will add red onions if I am using cabbage. For the 18-quart pot you will need at least 3 gallons of spring water available, ⅔ of the vessel's total capacity. Herbs and spices are a big part of the fun you will have in cooking, and here is where personal choice comes in. My advice is to do what you want, put in the herbs that you like. Just smell every herb before you put it in; it has to mix in your head first, and seem right to you.

One of the few actual measures I use is the *pinch* for herbs and spices; so here is a description:

> Small pinch: thumb and one finger.
> Large pinch: thumb and two fingers.
> Big pinch: still more fingers.

When it comes to the vegetables, I chop them roughly in large chunks or cut on the long bias to get more flavor.

Turkey Stock: Nice Carcass, Gobble Gobble

A turkey carcass or skeleton is perfect for a poultry stock, especially from a roasted bird, and is often available after a turkey meal as well. Don't forget the jelled drippings; otherwise you lose the gelatin you would derive from the raw bones. This stock can do the same thing that veal bones can do: (1) render gelatin from the joints; and (2) render a warm savory light golden broth. The fact that I am a son of New England where that turkey dinner tradition was born makes it particularly work for me.

CORE INGREDIENTS	SPICES
whole turkey carcass	allspice berries
pan drippings	black and white peppercorns
3 gallons spring water	nutmeg

ADDITIONAL VEGETABLES	HERBS
celery	thyme
carrot	marjoram
parsnip	parsley
butternut squash	sage
onion	
garlic	

If the turkey bones are raw, then roast them until golden brown. Cleave the largest joints before roasting. Put pan drippings and water in the pot. Add to the pot the rough chopped vegetables: one full bunch of celery, about four each of carrots and parsnips, half a peeled butternut squash, at least two onions, and four garlic bulbs. For spice add about four allspice berries, a large pinch of both peppercorns, and a small pinch of nutmeg. Add a bouquet of all the herbs, enough to fill a small fist.

Once it reaches a boil immediately turn down to a simmer, and simmer for at least 2½ hours. A ladle is good to skim off the unwanted flotsam and jetsam that float to the top. In the process of skimming you make friends with your stock and stay close. Strain into a large clean container with a 4-gallon capacity that can handle heat and is good for storing food. Voila!

Lobster Stock: *Out of the Sea for Me*

This is my favorite stock. There is so much right about this stock. Lobster shells and dulse seaweed right from our Maine coast locale: flavors straight from our sea and shore. It blows away all the classic stocks for elegance of flavor. Versatile, it can be used as a broth for noodles, a lobster essence reduction for a sauce, or as lobster ketchup.

CORE INGREDIENTS	SPICES
roasted lobster shells	paprika
clarified butter	saffron or osfor
3 gallons spring water	black and white peppercorns
	allspice or star anise

ADDITIONAL VEGETABLES	HERBS
celery	thyme
carrot	tarragon
fennel	sage
zucchini	parsley
plum tomatoes	
garlic	
ginger	
onion	
dulse seaweed	

The lobster shells have lots of flavor, and around New England you can always come by plenty of lobster shells. The trick is in getting the flavor out. Coat the lobster shells by using a brush to paint them with clarified butter. Then roast them until you can smell the roasting aroma, about 25 minutes. Now place shells in a pot with the water and the vegetables, cut on the bias this time. One bunch celery, six or more carrots, one stalk of fennel, one zucchini, six or more split plum tomatoes, four smashed heads of garlic, a few slivers of ginger, and two onions split in halves or quarters depending on size. Add a big pinch of dulse, a big pinch of paprika, a little pinch of saffron or a large pinch of osfor (the "poor man's saffron"), the peppercorns, four allspice berries or one star of anise. (Be careful with the anise, it is strong; if you aren't on familiar terms with anise, stick with allspice.) A generous full fist of the herbs mixed together: thyme, tarragon, sage, and parsley—goes in last. Again, low and slow for the cooking, simmering for at least 3 hours. It will come out a deep red. Strain and store as usual.

Vegan Vegetable-Seaweed Stock: From the Galley

This is the most versatile of all the stocks. Its simple earthy taste can back up any sauce, sauté, risotto, or soup. Seaweed gives it natural salts and makes it crisp. It is perfect for noodles in broth.

CORE INGREDIENTS	SPICES
roasted onions	paprika
roasted plum tomatoes w/ olive oil	turmeric
	Sichuan peppers
kombu seaweed	white peppercorns
3 gallons spring water	

ADDITIONAL VEGETABLES	HERBS
carrot	flat parsley
celery	tarragon
parsnip	
garlic	
ginger	

Roast about three or four onions at 400 degrees Fahrenheit. Split six to twelve plum tomatoes and roast them with a little olive oil until they are caramelized. Put onions and tomatoes in the pot of spring water and add four to eight stalks of kombu seaweed. Then add slivers of six carrots, one stalk of celery, two parsnips, and three smashed garlic bulb heads. Cut six slices of fresh ginger root and throw those in too. Then comes a large pinch of paprika, a small pinch of turmeric, a small pinch of Sichuan pepper, and a large pinch of white peppercorns; finally, add a nice small fist-sized bunch of parsley and tarragon.

This one you want to be a light broth, so don't cook it longer than 1½–2 hours. Check the taste often and turn if off quickly once it gets to the flavor you like. Drain and store as per usual. As with most vegan dishes, this will last in the refrigerator longer than animal-based stocks, perhaps ten days or more. Good luck!

8
In the Back of the House: Let's Make Some Soup!

The descriptions of soup that follow are all for large batches, for-a-gathering type soup. When I make a soup it's a lot: enough to make at least fifty full hearty bowls of soup. No matter how small it starts out, it seems to expand. Plus, as a restaurant chef with people showing up, you have to know how to make something out of nothing—and "poof"—soup becomes gourmet soup. So, let us start with a big pot, with room to expand from large to extra large. There is no sense in making a little once you set up to make soup. Soup pots that are home and café/diner size run from 12–32 quarts. The smallest I will use is 18 quarts; it is the one I use at home. Get the tall version and it should fit comfortably on any (gas!) stove: heavy bottomed, stainless steel, and copper-lined bottom for smooth, slow heat. Let the size of the pot determine your measures of the ingredients. A working chef mostly uses his or her eyes to measure when making a variety of soups and sauces all lined up on a ten-burner restaurant stove. We throw in as much food as the pot can handle well. Using speed and accuracy, we estimate the portions of raw food by using sight and smell. And, like a baseball pitcher, you keep all your pitches within an imaginary strike zone. Good food usually ensues.

An 18-quart soup pot will give you the room to make a 3–4 gallon batch of soup. The room to expand on the recipe is essential in true soup making. The French have a term for this, *potages de campagne* ("country soup"), which is the creative version, the preferred method. It can be determined by a scarcity of one food and an abundance of another; it summons the ingenuity of the chef. Unfortunately, too many restaurants are using the other method, *potages de réception*, meaning studied or thought-out soups. Many restaurants in America today have caught the "fast food virus" and are not into the art of soup. If you get a decent soup from them it is usually made two states over by a large company "specializing" in giving soups that original homemade, rough effect. Confusing, isn't it? If you get off on being lied to, or like me consider it entertainment, go to a supermarket and start reading the labels on the packaging.

So, I guess, now that we are back at the kitchen and in the back of the house, we should *get at it*. Here are some random chef tips that will distract you so you can get at it just a little later:

Use the following:
spring water
whole grains and beans
local sea salt and seaweed
local and/or organic vegetables
animals and seafood close to home (not the cat)
fresh spices and herbs alive with oils

Also:
Miso is a great bouillon for soup.
Give soup to your friends in winter.
Cold soup is not soup—just stuff you're too lazy to heat up—
    and gazpacho is a dip as far as I am concerned.
Fresh herbs and sea salt at the end of soup making can bring
    everything out.
Leftover rice, barley, and beans can turn a light soup into a
    hearty soup.
Riced potatoes can give creaminess to a broth.

50

Shoyu tamari soy sauce can give depth and body that vegans
crave after being cut off from beef stock.
Keep a garlic and salt paste, because who can't use more garlic?

Okay, now let's make some soup!

Black Bean Soup: "Black Gold, Texas Tea"

Black bean soup is one of America's tavern and pub staples. Topped
with sour cream, scallions, and hot sauce, it is deep, dark, and delicious;
and it is good for your heart and blood sugar levels. Whether it is cooked
Tex-Mex, Chinese, or Cuban style, what makes it popular is the deep
dark liquor that comes from slow-cooking the beans. The bean water
becomes the stock for the soup, and holds up to spice and hot peppers
very well. Cook the beans low and slow and develop the flavor with
herbs and spices. Black beans have a velvety, smoky flavor and hold
shape well during cooking.

CORE INGREDIENTS
black beans (turtle)
3 gallons spring water
sea salt
nori seaweed
olive oil or safflower oil

ADDITIONAL VEGETABLES
garlic
carrot
parsnip
celery
butternut squash
onion
ginger

SPICES
star anise
paprika
cumin
turmeric
chipotle
cayenne
allspice
coriander
tamari *(optional)*
Tabasco, green chili, or Thai red
    chili *(optional)*

HERBS
bay leaves
cilantro
basil
oregano

First the beans. Black beans need a 2.5 (or 3) to 1 ratio of spring water for a pot of beans with sauce; for soup it is more like 3 or 4 to 1. You'll decide how thick you want the soup and it can be adjusted at the end of cooking.

Before cooking, rinse the beans. For an 18-quart pot start with 3–4 quarts of beans and 3 gallons of spring water. You can soak the beans overnight or use the quick method I use because I often forget the overnight soak. Bring the beans and spring water to a boil. Turn off the heat and let stand for 2 hours. You'll see that the beans have expanded. Do this a second time in the same water, but this time add some spice—a couple of cloves of garlic, one or two star anise, two bay leaves, two large pinches each of paprika and cumin, one large pinch each of turmeric, chipotle, cayenne, allspice, and coriander. Bring to a boil and let stand one more hour. They should pretty much be done but still firm at this point.

Note: Bring to a boil is *not* boiling—you are putting the beans on high ascending heat, then turning the heat off just before it really boils; that way the beans won't split. Boiling is for mashed potatoes and pasta, not stews and soups.

Next, or actually while the beans are cooking, take 2 pounds of carrots, 1 pound of parsnips, ½ pound heart of celery, one half of a good-sized butternut squash, peel, and cut into a medium-small dice or half-moon slivers. Also, cut 2 pounds of onion into small dice and mince eight cloves of garlic and 2 ounces of ginger. (Mince and dice are actually just what they sound like; no explanation will make it clearer.)

Toss all of this together in a large mixing bowl. Add a small pinch each of cayenne, turmeric, cumin, and coriander. Also, add one bunch of fresh cilantro, rough chopped, and ¼ cup each of minced basil and oregano. Mix together the vegetables, spices, and herbs; add three large pinches of salt, ¼ cup chopped nori seaweed, and let stand to mingle the spices and flavors. Salt cooks things too. Get a wok or sauté pan hot, add in olive oil or safflower oil, and quick sauté all the ingredients together the way you would with a vegetable curry. Cook until al dente—8 minutes? I don't wear a watch.

Add your sautéed vegetables to the black beans and then simmer the soup, a slow light simmer, for up to one hour. Should you add more heat and salt? Taste it first; then decide. For salting there is tamari; dark soy goes good with black beans, even Chinese mushroom soy. For peppering there is Tabasco, green chili, and Thai red chili. I have some hot sauce I bought called "Pain."

Other good garnishes are: sour cream, yogurt, fresh cilantro and scallion, roasted pumpkin seeds. All this is a nice trip into original cuisine, tribal even. This bean variety originated from Peru. So watch it, it could be addictive.

Onion Soup with Miso: East Meets West in the Onion Patch

The image that onion soup conjures up is a French beefy broth with a slab of melted cheese on top: this is not that. We got rid of the cow and brought out the new headliner—the flavor of caramelized onions. We take these yummy browned onions and match them with a classic miso broth. Caramelize? This is basically braising the onions slowly to bring out the sugars and brown them. Which onions? Use any combination you want—white, Spanish, yellow, etc.—just as for stocks; you can even add slivers of shallots or leeks. My personal favorite onion for this soup is Vidalia.

CORE INGREDIENTS

onions
clarified butter and olive oil
3 gallons vegan vegetable-
    seaweed stock (see
    chapter 7)
miso, sweet white and dark

ADDITIONAL VEGETABLES

potato (optional)
garlic (optional)

SPICES

sea salt
nutmeg
white and black pepper
allspice berries (crushed)
tamari
mushroom soy sauce

HERBS

tarragon
thyme
marjoram
parsley

53

First thing—*the thing:* onions. You can get as much as 10 pounds of onions or more in our 4½ gallon pot. But with too much onion they will poach, not braise and caramelize properly. So start with 6–8 pounds.

Slicing: Cut the onion ends off, split into half-moons, and peel. Slice the half-moons into thin, long half-moon ribbons. Not paper-thin—you need something to braise. Toss it all into a large mixing bowl. Add two large pinches of salt, one large pinch of nutmeg, two large pinches of white and black pepper combined, and eight crushed allspice berries. Mix, then let it rest for a minute. Get your pot hot by leaving it on low to medium heat for a few minutes. You want heat already in the soup pot because all the onions are going to pull the heat right out and stall the sauté right away.

Sauté, then braise, then simmer: When you are ready to do the first step—sauté—turn the heat up high, cover the bottom of the pot with clarified butter and/or olive oil, and quickly toss in onion mix; with paddle ready, start stirring and cooking onions. The high heat starts the browning process and sears the spice into the onion. Keep stirring with the paddle at this temperature for about 10 minutes: browning, not burning. Black is bitter.

If the caramelizing builds up too much on the bottom of the pan and threatens to turn too dark, deglaze by adding some of the vegetable stock. "Deglaze" is another term that sounds like what it is—defeat the glaze by adding liquid, rendering it into a sauce. And now that we have added the liquid and reduced the heat, we are braising. At this time, add the fresh herbs, tarragon, thyme, and marjoram—minced—about one tablespoon each. The braising continues the caramelizing. Braise by turning the heat down to a more moderate level. Go low and slow to bring out the sugars. It will take at least 20–30 minutes. Keep adding stock as you need it to keep the onions braising, thus creating a smooth, light brown syrup. A good trick is to put a round cut piece of parchment paper resting right on the onions so they will sweat right into the braise. After the onions are finished braising, add the remainder of the 3 gallons of vegan stock. Bring to a boil and then simmer slowly for about one hour.

You'll finish it off with miso paste. You don't want to boil or cook miso very long—it ruins it. So, we add it in the end. Take 4–5 cups total of light and dark miso combined and whip it into some of the onion soup in a separate container. Pour that mixture back into the soup. Bring to temperature and taste. If you need more salt or heartiness, splash in some tamari and mushroom soy sauce—it will blend immediately and need no cooking. Garnish with fresh chopped parsley to serve.

Some onion soup notes:

Popular in Roman Times as a way of feeding the poor and thought to be a restorative (you know, aphrodisiac).

The modern version of it started in the eighteenth century in Paris. To excite the Libertines.

You can use sherry to deglaze but I think it hides the onion flavor; dark beer is great, though.

If you miss the roux from the classic version, add potatoes (1–2 pounds for this amount of soup.) There are two good ways to do this:

- Boil the potatoes with garlic and rice into the finished soup before you add the miso.
- Cut small potato slivers and add while braising the onions to dissolve.

You want to serve bread with soup most of the time anyway, but with this soup you really want to serve bread; just about any kind will do fine. Have it your way.

Lobster Broth with Tofu and Julienned Vegetables: Royalty from the Gulf of Maine

In my kitchen this is the king of broths. It is versatile with a depth of flavor that can include other foods, though you don't want to crowd it with strong flavors; that is why I chose a light white miso and tofu for this broth. The only history I know about lobster stock is my own. Years ago I could not find a lobster stock recipe anywhere. Cooking in Boston we knew a lot about lobster, but I never saw anyone save shells for stock. I followed the method used for other stocks and started roasting the shells—it brings out the oils. This is a good soup to make to experience the elegant flavor that gets packed into a well-prepared lobster stock.

CORE INGREDIENTS	SPICES
3½ gallons lobster stock (see chapter 7)	turmeric
	coriander
sesame or safflower oil	paprika and smoked
dulse, smoked	paprika
tofu	cayenne
white miso	cumin
	sea salt
ADDITIONAL VEGETABLES	
	HERBS
carrots	
parsnips	tarragon
zucchini	cilantro
scallions	optional garnishes (see
fennel	below)
ginger	

The broth from the lobster stock already has plenty of character, but I want a little more intensity of flavor for this soup. Since the lobster essence is the main star in this soup, we will give it a spotlight by using it for a reduction.

First strain the cold stock through a fine sieve (strainer). You don't want any debris, just pure stock. Now, get it on the stove to reduce. With 3½ gallons of stock, you would want to reduce it to 3 gallons or when you think it is intense enough. Don't jump the gun and add flavor—wait for it to come out. The heat should be intense enough to "let off steam"; that's what makes the reduction.

Meanwhile, cut your vegetables. The julienne cut is like a matchstick, except longer, and sometimes bigger, but not any thinner. For root vegetables, like carrots or even zucchini, the first step is to cut long slices on the bias. Then stack the oblong slices and cut into long matchsticks.

Peel, slice, and julienne 2 pounds of carrots, 1 pound of parsnip, 1 pound of zucchini, and 1 pound of fennel root. Mince 3 ounces of ginger root and toss it all into a mixing bowl. Then throw in the spices and herbs—one big pinch each of turmeric, coriander, paprika and smoked paprika and one small pinch of cayenne, and cumin; then two large pinches of salt. Add the fresh herbs—tarragon and cilantro, ¼ cup of each minced. Toss it all and then let it sit.

Now it is time for a quick sauté or stir-fry. Take your julienne vegetable/spice/herb mix and throw it into the biggest, hottest fry pan or wok that you have. Cook fast and hot in sesame or safflower oil—just enough to wilt the vegetables. Add this to the reduced broth along with 2–3 tablespoons of chopped smoked dulse and 1–2 pounds of cubed tofu. Bring to temperature. Put 3 cups of white miso paste into a mixing bowl, add enough broth to make a slurry, and pour the slurry back into the soup. Let the soup sit on low temperature for 5–10 minutes.

This soup can take a number of garnishes:
> noodles—soba, angel hair
> minced scallion and cilantro
> hot sauce and roasted chili
> oils—toasted sesame, olive oil
> slivers of red and yellow peppers
> and, of course, lobster meat, however much you can
> > come by or afford

Cream of Roasted Mushroom: No Alice, Not That Kind of Mushroom

This is an earthy, yet elegant soup. A French favorite, it could go well on a noble's table or in a wooden bowl at a street stall in Paris. Roasting the mushroom concentrates the musky earth marrow taste of the mushrooms. I use crimini in this recipe but white mushrooms are good, shitake are brilliant, and portabella are like meat itself. There could be multiple versions. Remember to save the juices from the roasting pan—that is pure flavor for your puree.

CORE INGREDIENTS

assorted mushrooms
olive oil
3 gallons turkey stock or
    vegetable stock (see
    chapter 7)
chickpea miso

ADDITIONAL VEGETABLES

onion
Yukon potatoes
Parsnip
celery root
celery
butternut squash
garlic

SPICES

nutmeg
allspice berries, crushed
black and white pepper
sea salt
turmeric

HERBS

tarragon
thyme
sage

Oh, by the way: the "cream" base for this soup is non-dairy; it was what I adapted to stay vegan yet honor a request for "cream" of tomato soup as described in chapter 3. It is a puree with potatoes and root vegetable as its base. Peel and rough cube (two inch) 2–3 pounds of onions, 4 pounds of potatoes (Yukon!), 2–3 pounds of parsnip, one whole celery root (celeriac), half a head of celery—about 2 pounds—and 1 pound of butternut squash for color. Add ten cloves of garlic, finely chopped. Toss all the vegetables, except onion, into a bowl and add spice; one large pinch nutmeg, eight berries of crushed allspice, one big pinch (four fingers) white and black pepper, one big pinch of turmeric, two big pinches of sea salt. Toss. We are making a vegetable puree, so we need to start with a sauté and braise of the onions and garlic. We could boil everything then puree, but there is no fun or flavor in that. We are going to caramelize the vegetables more lightly than we did for the onion soup; here we are looking for a light caramel—a blond caramelizing—that's it.

Braise the onions for 15 minutes, add the remaining vegetables, and continue to braise until the outside of the potato starts to fall into the braised mix. Then, add the fresh herbs, ¼ cup total combination of minced tarragon, thyme, and sage, and cook for 5 minutes longer before the next step.

Meanwhile, take 4–6 pounds of mushrooms, put them in whole in a roasting pan, add a few slivers of garlic, two small pinches of the mixed herbs, one big pinch of salt, and a few drizzles of olive oil, and roast them for about 25 minutes.

Now we can finish the soup. I usually add a vegetable stock packed with garlic, making this a vegan soup. (Or you could use a turkey stock like the one we made back in chapter 7.) So now that our soup has a nice braise on, add 2–3 gallons of turkey stock. Throw in a handful of the roasted whole mushrooms, plus the mushroom juice. Bring to a boil and let simmer for about 30 minutes or until the vegetables are completely soft.

Meanwhile, slice the remaining mushrooms. When the soup is done, it is ready to puree. Add two cups of chickpea miso, drop in an immersion blender, then pulverize it until it is cream. Magic cream of mushroom—add the sliced mushrooms for texture contrast. If you are totally bent on dairy food, add a dollop of crème fraiche and minced chive.

Other garnishes are:

> parsley
> chervil

That's it. This soup you want to taste as is.

9
May:
Taking the Soup Kitchen Public

Now that Bill and Larry had a mission statement on the table so to speak, it was time to let the cat out of the bag and meet the press. They arranged for Nan Lincoln of the *Bar Harbor Times* to do an interview in Bill's kitchen, and she did a feature story on the soup kitchen which appeared in the April 23 issue of the weekly paper: a full spread on page five. It was entitled "Fearless Optimism in a Bowl of Soup" and had a cartoon drawing of a bowl of soup with steam coming off of it in the center of the header with a smiling Larry to the left and a kind of fierce-looking Bill in a hooded sweatshirt

Jennie Cline. She volunteered to set up the Common Good Web site, which gave it a public presence that was crucial for its development.

on the right. They could not have asked for better press at that point. There was no mad stampede to Bill's kitchen door for soup afterwards though, as they thought might happen. Nor did anyone from Northeast Harbor or anywhere else drop a check in the mail for, say, fifty thousand dollars because they were so inspired. But some other lower key but still very important things did happen as a result of this article.

The first came in a most unexpected form, a note to Larry and Fran from their eleven-year-old granddaughter Emma, down in Huntsville, Alabama. Not an e-mail as one might expect from a contemporary eleven-year-old whose father works in hi tech, but an old-fashioned handwritten note card, in purple pen:

Dear Papa Larry and Granny Franny:

Thank you so much for the birthday check. My mom said I had to put half of it in the bank though. That was kind of disappointing. Well, today we got the soup story. That was so cool! I hope you have fun with that. I can't wait till May when we go to New York. That will be so much fun. I can't wait to see everybody. Well, it's late and I got to get to bed, I miss you. Bye!

Love, Emma

First of all, this tickled Larry immensely as he thought of using "that was kind of disappointing" as a mantra when things went wrong. Like, "A huge deer jumped in front of my car and I couldn't stop in time and it scared the bejesus out of everyone in the car and destroyed the Subaru's front end, *that was kind of disappointing*"; or, "I came home and found a note that my girlfriend had run off to Costa Rica with my best friend, *that was kind of disappointing.*" It had a ring to it, a wryness that could take the sting out of bad news that was, well, kind of disappointing.

This mantra helped as things unfolded. But more important still was the other side of the little card on which Emma, a budding artist, had drawn a small picture with the same purple pen. It had a rectangular pot with a handle and steam lines coming out of it and the word soup below, with an arrow pointing to the pot and the words *slurp!* and *yumm!* printed on either side. It was cute and spunky and invigorating. Larry showed it to Bill the next day—"That's our logo!" said Bill.

Larry concurred. He had his artist friend Nancy Diedrickson copy it over in India ink and add Common Good Soup Kitchen & Co-op inside the pot, and the rest is history. The very fact that it was Nancy that did it was a testimony to the power of the Common Good community to bring people together: she did this in spite of the fact that she and Bill had experienced a major "episode of conflict" the previous year when Nancy was a food

The Common Good Soup Kitchen logo

server at a café where Bill was the chef. This image became their symbol, their visual icon: on the walls of the soup kitchen space, on their flyers, on their letterhead, on their Web page, in all their ad copy, in the newspaper headlines for their press releases, and eventually on Larry's left forearm as his first tattoo at the ripe young age of seventy-one.

Then there was Jennie Cline. Six days after the newspaper article appeared Larry received an e-mail from her that said in part, "I am semi-retired and looking for Web projects that are not terribly demanding. I would love to set up and maintain a page for you, if that is of any interest. Besides donating my time to do that, I would absorb the cost of a mutually agreed upon domain name and host it appropriately—and maintain it."

"If that is of any interest?!" thought Larry, "Holy Jumpin' Jehosophat!" Larry knew they needed to have a Web site and was hoping down the line they could wangle one somehow. Now came this, totally out of the blue. This e-mail is also a microcosm of two things that kept happening with the project: (1) people somehow appearing, stepping up at the right time to provide the resources that were needed to move things forward; and (2) people just hearing about the program and becoming eager to make suggestions, chip in ideas, many of which turned out, in one way or the other, to come to fruition. Jennie was more than true to her word; she put together a first class web site with beautiful graphics, all kinds of links, very spiffy and professional. It was way beyond the basic start up utilitarian site that people expected. Larry loved to watch people's eyes go wide when they said to him, as so many did over the following weeks: "You should have a Web site."

"Actually," Larry would reply as matter-of-factly as he could, "we have one already, www.commongoodsoupkitchen.org, check it out." Then they checked it out and were *really* impressed. Of course all the content had to come from Larry; he found that the hours from 3–6 a.m. were generally not otherwise occupied and that the six hours of sleep he generally got from 9 p.m. to 3 a.m. were sufficient, so that was when the Web site content was transmitted, and when lots of other Common Good Soup Kitchen documents were produced as well. Jennie also brought more than thirty distinctively different artistic bowls from the Andover School Pottery program, where her husband taught, up to Maine with her and they hit just the right note in gracing the tables of the Common Good Café and Soup Kitchen space when it materialized later that summer.

Notwithstanding all of this activity, the bare facts were that at this point in time the project consisted of two old dudes whose heads buzzed with enthusiasm, a mission statement, a Web site, and about one hundred bucks in the bank. They needed to find a space, raise some money, and get more folks involved, if anything was to really happen. The word of mouth about the soup and the newspaper article and the mission statement generated enough local interest to get a fund-raiser scheduled at the local congregational church, which had a kitchen. They had a kind of "in" there as well as Bill had helped them do the cooking for their own annual spaghetti dinner fund-raiser for the food pantry. It was on for the last weekend in May, a Saturday night supper, with a suggested donation of ten dollars in the bowl, hoping for more of course.

Meanwhile, Bill needed some new volunteers to help with the weekly chopping and peeling as his winter helpers were starting to find employment. So Larry reached out to his friend and neighbor Janice, who had a long history of volunteering for good causes in the community, and his friend Ruth Roberts, a very spry octogenarian who had grown up in Maine on the remote island of Vinylhaven. She was willing to write out labels for Bill's soup and salad containers each week, thus relieving Bill of that chore. The next week she in turn brought her friend Ruth Jellison, who helped with the labels and eventually did some chopping and peeling too. Bill contacted some of his old waitstaff, too. So now there was a volunteer nucleus forming, a chopping crew, that showed up at Bill's kitchen and helped prep for the weekly soups and salads. Joni Roths, a local resident whose family had been in Southwest Harbor since before the American Revolution and who really knew a lot of the old-timers, was on board as a regular delivery person, ferreting out those who could use some soup and empathic conversation—and so "soup with soul" deliveries emerged.

Larry and Bill also put together a small advisory board to help build the fledgling program and to give it some additional creditability. There was Fay Lawson, a Hancock County Commissioner with a resume of public service as long as your arm, and a good friend of Larry's for many years. There was Annie Dundon, a physician's assistant, mother of two, well-known citizen, and a general co-op enthusiast. Jim King, a local innkeeper with keen civic interests and a longstanding friendship with Bill, was the third board member. Dr. Geoff Knowles, a local chiropractor who was also an expert in nutrition and health and very passionate about it, was drawn to the project and became the fourth member. Also on board was Peter Golbitz, the soybean guru who had been into natural/organic foods for years and consulted about soybean use all over the globe. Soon afterwards, Jennie Cline agreed to serve on the advisory board as well.

Bill and Larry felt things were getting "real" enough to start looking at possible locations for the café/co-op soup kitchen. They initially looked at two possible spots: a building in Town Hill, a village at the center of Mount Desert Island, fifteen minutes away from Southwest Harbor; and a second building in town that would be shared with a local business, Chow Maine. There were possibilities there, but also serious limitations. The Town Hill building had no kitchen and would require a lot of renovation and the Chow Maine space had only a small kitchen and was expensive. They still needed to find a suitable space and sufficient funds to rent it.

There was a whole other line of activity related to the project developing at the same time as well; a fugue and toccata of its own in what was becoming a polyphonic panoply of planning. It related to the business model, the organizational structure, and "the general on the ground." Bill and Larry were both aware of the fact that if they were actually to launch the café/co-op/soup kitchen they would need a general on the ground, someone to literally mind the store, keep the books and so on. Bill would have his hands full with the food planning, purchasing, and preparing end; Larry already had more than his hands full on the organizing and pamphleteering end, and in any event the store could not be minded from 3 a.m. to 6 a.m., which was the bulk of the time that Larry had available for the project. Larry was keenly aware of the fact that his primary domestic responsibilities took priority during daylight hours. Larry said that he could be the Thomas Paine of the revolution, rallying support among the populace and papering the village with pamphlets, while Bill as George Washington could oversee the overall food and business strategy; but they still needed some other officers, brigadier generals if you will, to carry the program forward, or at least one!

So, they thought of James Tarnow. James had run a local coffee shop, Jumpin Java, for a number of years, and had a degree in finance. Bill and Larry had both hung out at Jumpin Java a lot, and knew James well. James had sold the shop back in '06 when he lost his lease, and though he had moved to Portland since, he was only employed seasonally down there and might be available to come up and be their man on the ground. James was sufficiently interested, had sufficient time and was sufficiently committed to helping his friend Larry, to do a lot of background development work on his computer down in Portland. He researched co-ops, mining various Web sites. The e-mails and phone conversations flew back and forth along the length of the coast of Maine between Larry and James. What kind of benefits would the co-op members receive? Would there be discounts, rebates or both? How would the membership program be structured? How would all of this tie in with the profit-making aspect of things? James talked to Bill and put together a business plan, based on Bill's estimates of the food he could produce and James's estimates of operating costs.

Larry knew that he also needed to work out the organizational details much more precisely now: could they set up a nonprofit, charitable organization that would operate a business, i.e. the café and market, for its own benefit? How would this all relate to the co-op component and the soup kitchen? Bill was partly of a mind to be totally entrepreneurial: just open a natural food café and market as a business. But he also recognized along with Larry that the word "co-op" had a lot of magic for people, that lots of people were enthusiastic about the idea of having a local co-op, and that they might lose this base of support if they did not have a co-op structure. Larry in turn was totally committed to the idea that in order to have a viable co-op and soup kitchen in this community that was so sparsely populated in winter, they had to have the two income streams: the sale of food to the tourists and summer residents in the season, and donations from residents who were relatively affluent and had a stake in supporting the community. The café and store alone could not support the program because sales would be so dead in the winter and it would take years, if it could ever be done, to build a charitable base big enough to support the operation on its own. The question was how to structure the two-income stream organization, and Larry knew that he had to seek out expertise to guide them.

Peter Roy, Esq. was a local attorney with offices in downtown Ellsworth, the commercial hub of down east Maine. Larry had liked Peter since the first day they had met. He had gone with Franny to see Peter on a real estate matter, and Franny was upset with Larry because he had just come out of the woods, walking the dog in winter, and had not tied the laces in his boots. She apologized for this to Peter as they were introduced and ushered into the conference room and Peter turned to her and said, "Not to worry, Fran, this is down east Maine, most of my clients don't even *have* laces in their boots." Peter had a great sense of humor and though they had ended up consulting him on a variety of fairly serious matters, Larry and Fran had always left his office smiling; he also had a reputation for being tough and tenacious and winning a lot more than losing.

Larry explained the project to Peter, who asked a lot of general questions before they got down to the legalities. He was bemused, and took the hard-headed skeptic's approach: "A co-op eh? I love to go the Blue Hill co-op. People pick up a head of organic broccoli and stare at it and a dreamy look comes into their eyes: 'Oh look, broccoli,' they coo tenderly." He cupped his hands and looked at the imaginary broccoli with mock tenderness, mimicking the action as he spoke. On the legal side, when he somewhat reluctantly got there, Peter said that he could quickly and easily incorporate the soup kitchen and co-op as a non-profit organization in Maine, but that getting federal tax exempt status was a more complex and expensive process, one that he would actually farm out to an accounting colleague who specialized in such things. He also suggested that Larry and Bill might be able to work with the Maine Community Foundation, which made grants to support such do-good projects as theirs and might be able to be a fiscal sponsor while the federal tax-exempt status was pending. As to the relationship between the business end and the charitable end, operating the café to make money to support the co-op and the soup kitchen, he would have to consult with some folks who specialized in such matters. Larry went home and put Peter on his list to receive all e-mailed information about the doings of the Common Good: he needed to keep their attorney in the loop, and also enjoyed the thought of Peter continuing to read about his "dreamy-eyed" do-gooder activities.

At last the date of the first fund-raiser for the Common Good arrived; unfortunately, Larry and Fran were away on a family trip to New York that weekend. This was inconvenient, but Bill and the volunteer crew handled it well. Larry had a stand-in: Eli, aka Dr. Elias Barlia, a Jewish/Cuban tractor driver/psychologist/animal behavior therapist. Eli, whom Larry had known for over forty years, had recently gone through hard times and was out in Maine to spend some time with Larry and Fran for recuperation, regrouping, and reflection. As it happened, Eli and Larry had talked on and off over the years about how cool it would be to open a coffee shop, a community hangout, and Eli was very intrigued by what Larry and Bill were cooking up. He helped out with the fund-raiser as a stand-in for Larry. Bill made some delicious soups and some veggie sushi rolls, Ruth and Ruth were at the door to collect donations and give out information, and copies of the mission statement and a shorter summary about the program were available. Saturday night Larry called back to Maine and talked to Eli to get the report. The fund-raiser had gone well, and they had taken in around four hundred dollars; the food was great; the vibes were very good; even Bill got up and talked briefly but eloquently. The turnout was about forty or so, less than Larry had hoped for, but all in all it was good, a good start. Now there was in fact a bit of money in the bank to keep the soup coming.

Out in New York that weekend, Larry and Franny were celebrating: their son Andy, who had worked for nonprofit organizations and good causes all his adult life, was receiving a major award for his good works. Larry was excited about his son's award, excited about spending the weekend in the company of his favorite cousins and two of his grandchildren, and excited about the prospects for the Common Good Co-op and Soup Kitchen fund-raiser that weekend. Andrew told him that he had made contact with some of the nonprofit legal types he knew in Maine and they would be getting in touch with Larry to help him consult on the nonprofit organizational issues that had arisen for Larry and Bill. Larry thanked him heartily. It was then that he realized that his son was kind of "Mr. Nonprofit" and really knew a lot about all this stuff. He was in fact now following in his son's footsteps!

The next day something happened that made Larry feel that the karma of this thing was following him and that his fate was sealed. He took Franny to a matinee movie, a big city treat and a time for Larry to forget about the Common Good project entirely for a while. They went to see a romantic comedy with Jennifer Aniston called *VIP.* "A nice light diversion," thought Larry. In a critical scene where the protagonists are getting to know one another more intimately over dinner, the man asks the woman how she likes her job, and she is lukewarm, more or less saying it's a living; it does not excite her, but she doesn't really expect more. He asks her to stretch herself, to tell him what she would be doing if she could do anything she wanted: her dream job. She doesn't do that kind of fantasizing, so she demurs, but he cajoles, asks her to just try it, let it come to her, imagine it. She closes her eyes, gets a dreamy look on her face, and says: "I would be running a full-service soup kitchen."

The hairs on Larry's neck all stood up, and his spine tingled. Generally he was not a strong believer in fate, but this coincidence was too much. He was sure now there was no walking away; the soup kitchen was his destiny.

10
June:
The Seawall Saga

The Common Good Co-op and Soup Kitchen

What is it? Where will it be? When will it be?
How did it come to be? How can I be part of it?
What will it do for me? What can I do for it?
Exactly who is going to be doing exactly what?

Find out the answers and more:
Public Information and Discussion Meeting
Southwest Harbor Public Library
Saturday, June 6, 4–6 p.m.
Light refreshments will be served.
All invited.

Larry emailed this flyer to everyone he could think of that might be interested, utilizing his senior college lists, his music lists, his croquet player lists, his poker player lists, his local friends lists, and his small list of soup kitchen volunteers and board members so far. He printed out hard copies and had his friends Ruth and Janice plaster them all over town. Eli was gone on a fly-fishing jaunt again, but James agreed to come up for the weekend

Dave and Vickie Lloyd. The soup kitchen angels; owners of the Seawall Motel and the adjoining restaurant space that gave the soup kitchen a home.

and see what it was all about. Bill was on board to do some refreshments. There would be wine, and Carolyn Dyer of the library staff had volunteered to help with the set up. This was it, the public information meeting he and Bill had been working toward since their very first walk and talk back in February. A lot had happened since then, and there was a lot of buzz, a lot of questions in the air as Bill and Larry met and greeted various folks around town.

Larry prepared a talk in which he would try to be totally open and transparent; he would actually use the bus analogy, invite people to get on the bus, and would say that as far as he was concerned that Bill was a Picasso of food. He would also say that they hoped that they would get funded and make money and that they could hire people, and pay decent wages and benefits, that working for a nonprofit did not mean working for meager wages as far as *he* was concerned. He would talk about the synergy of the elements in the program and even the more difficult ones to achieve, like breaking through the "brown rice" cultural barrier and working with local food producers as much as possible. He was ready for an upbeat, assertive type of presentation. As a former college professor he had given hundreds of talks and lectures in his life, maybe even thousands, but none had ever had more riding on it, as far as Larry was concerned, than this one.

He also prepared an information packet for everyone in attendance. This packet grew to seven pages, each one a self-contained "one pager" of some aspect of the program: an overview and summary statement of the Common Good Soup Kitchen and Co-op; a description of the free soup program emphasizing the novel, "soup with soul" delivery" component; information on the proposed Common Good Café and market; a summary of the business plan; information on the proposed co-op membership and benefits plan with a basic dues of twenty dollars per year; details on the various types of volunteers needed; and finally a sign up sheet for volunteers and contributors, which included the Paul Newman Club level—for a contribution of a thousand dollars or more you could work with Chef Bill to create a soup and name it yourself.

When the day arrived, Bill worked with James and a crew to get the refreshments going, while Larry worked to get the handouts printed up. He also used his computer to make an iron-on transfer of the Common Good logo and then pressed it on to a T-shirt, which was what he wore to give his talk. The library itself was an inspiration to Bill and Larry, a cozy place where they both enjoyed hanging out, and a small town establishment that had fairly easily raised a million dollars for renovations and improvement not that many years ago. The library staff members were also enthusiastic supporters of the soup kitchen/co-op, so all in all it was a good vibe place. With all the buzz going on around town from the mission statement, the newspaper article and such, Larry half expected (or dreamed of?) a jam-packed crowd he would have to thread through when he got there, but instead he found a modest audience of around thirty-five or so, many of whom were from the inner circle of Bill and Larry's friends and chopping and peeling volunteers. Were they preaching only to the already converted?

But there were a bunch of new faces, too. Larry was particularly heartened to see Dr. Julian Kuffler there with his wife. Dr. Kuffler was Larry and Franny's primary care physician, a man who not only treated his patients but also had worked tirelessly to improve health services for the community. Okay, crowd-wise they had not hit a home run, but it was at least a double, hit off the fabled green monster wall at Boston's Fenway Park. He gave the talk, it had a lot of humor, he outlined the bus trip metaphor, he kept it to twenty minutes or so, and no one asked any really difficult or embarrassing questions. The presence of a couple of farmers and lobstermen in the audience was revealed during the discussion period. A very high percentage of the folks there signed on to pledge contributions or be volunteers; those volunteer sheets were to be the true focus of moving forward to the next phase. If they had dug out the hole in April and May, now the concrete had been poured into the forms and they had a real foundation beneath them.

As he thought about it afterwards a subtle but significant shift occurred for Larry: he had been envisaging that the mission statement would mobilize the multitudes, so to speak, create an overwhelming outpouring of grassroots enthusiasm for the project. What he saw now was that they had mobilized a smaller cadre, the usual suspects plus some new folks that had signed up or shown up. It was with this cadre that they would have to work further to mobilize the multitudes. In a sense it was a bunch of friends or soon-to-be friends that would be in it together, building the program. He saw this now, and it was good.

The program continued to grow when Larry arranged for another fund-raiser, this one with musicians at Sips café in town, and Jennifer, the proprietor, offered to add 10 percent of the profits to the donation bowl take for that night. It was fun for Larry to tell Bill this, and see the look of surprise on Bill's face to hear that his former employer was aiding them in this manner. The fund-raiser at Sips café was a great success—the packed house that Larry had been hoping for, almost salivating over, finally materialized. The musicians, the customers, and the café staff all had a rollicking good time, there were lots of enthusiastic good wishes expressed about the project, a bunch of new volunteers signed up, and there was a good amount of cash in the straw basket as well. When the one-hundred-dollar check for the share of the profits was added into the kitty a week or so later, the total for the night stood at close to eight hundred dollars in donations. It dawned on Larry that his three and a half years as musical impresario for Sips was something that he could now draw on for the soup kitchen: his musician contacts would be great resources for soup kitchen fund-raisers and community events.

Meanwhile, back at Bill's kitchen, soup was still being produced and distributed every week, but following the fund-raisers there was now a cadre of new volunteer "choppers." Some of these folks turned out to be key players over the coming months. There was Arnold Weisenberg, a seventy-ish gentleman with gray hair, a short beard, and a ponytail. He showed up bearing his own set of knives neatly folded in a fabric case. With his considerable cooking experience and expertise, Arnold quickly became Bill's number one sous-chef. Then there was Leanne Nickon, who had formerly worked as a waitress for Bill and who soon after hearing about the project was happily chopping and peeling away on the back porch next to Bill's kitchen, a natural extension of the food preparation space in good weather. Leanne was also a talented baker, was interested in doing more for the co-op, and eventually would end up more or less keeping it alive during the summer. Other newcomers showed up, too: seasonal residents Jill Freundlich and Elaine Falcichio, local resident Carol Dow. "We have a community going here," Bill told Larry with some wonderment. "The volunteers *are* the co-op, it's here already in a way. The energy is incredible."

The volunteer sign up sheet had listed sous-chef/chopping, soup delivery, fund-raising, special events, membership, education, green projects, and "other" as options that people could check off. Larry was surprised to find that chopping was far and away the most popular volunteer activity. There were some volunteers for other categories though, as well. Ann and Mike Sanders, who lived right down the road from Larry and Fran, were particularly interesting because they wrote in that they would volunteer to do whatever was necessary. Ann had particular skills in software and Mike's strength was in hardware design. Ann readily agreed to design and print a brochure with content that Larry would provide. They also talked about setting up a tracking system for the co-op to monitor membership sales and such through the cash register. Larry got the info for the brochure done in the wee hours as usual, and in a day or so Ann got the brochure copy back to Larry, a very spiffy tri-fold with the program laid out, some key pictures and even a little space to sign up to volunteer to work for the Common Good.

Meanwhile, Larry and Bill had made some progress on locating a kitchen space: shortly before the library meeting Bill ran into Dave Lloyd at the local supermarket on the hill just outside of town. At that point Bill and Larry had been discussing a backup plan: if the resources/space to open a market and café did not materialize, they could possibly get going by at least having a commercial kitchen from which to operate, where soup kitchen product could be produced both for continued free delivery to seniors and for sale as a separate food line via distribution to retail outlets. So when Bill ran into Dave and Dave asked him how things were going and what was new, Bill said that he was looking for a kitchen. "Really?" said Dave. "It just so happens I have a kitchen that could be just what you are looking for." So, out of this chance meeting the Seawall Saga began.

Annabelle Robbins had been a long-standing local fixture in town, an iconic tough-minded independent Maine businessperson and civic-minded citizen. For many years she ran Annabelle's Seawall Dining Room and the adjacent Seawall Motel, which were located on a twelve-acre parcel of land overlooking the ocean adjacent to the Seawall section of Acadia National Park, just about three miles from the center of town. The natural seawall had created a freshwater pond and marsh just across the road from the ocean, and the restaurant and Annabelle's house were perched along the shores of this pond with a spectacular view of the surf and the rocky coast. Like almost everyone else in town over the age of twelve, Larry had been to the Seawall Dining Room more than once: it was a classic fried fish, chowder, lobster and steak establishment, a large space that could accommodate 150 or so diners, and was filled with tourists in the summer and utilized by locals for Christmas parties, high school reunions and other such events in the off-season. A local landmark, if you will, for nigh on thirty years or so. Larry had also spent many happy hours among the rocks and tide pools at the oceanfront there, as had countless others. In the early 1990s Annabelle sold the entire parcel and businesses to Dave and Vickie Lloyd, who came up from Connecticut. They ran the restaurant pretty much in the Annabelle mold for a few summers, but running a restaurant was not really their thing, nor were they prepared to provide the updates it would need to be more contemporary. So they turned the space into an artists' workshop for the summers, they operated the motel, they enjoyed the unparalleled beauty of living there, and people more or less forgot about it as a restaurant space except as something that used to be. As it happened, the artist workshop era had come to an end, and the space was vacant, commercial kitchen and all, for 2009 and no one as yet had stepped up to rent it. Dave was very supportive of the co-op/soup kitchen project as Bill described it, and he was sure that they could work out some kind of deal.

Shortly after the supermarket meeting there was a "Guess who I ran into today?" phone call from Bill to Larry, one of a long line of such phone calls with the same opening line that started in February of '09 and goes on between them to this day. Not long after that, Bill met Dave down at Seawall to look at the space. He reported to Larry that the space was really good: the kitchen was fully equipped and there was tons of stuff there—tables, chairs, bowls, plates, utensils, all of Annabelle's old stuff—and they could probably also rent part of the old restaurant space to create room for a small café and market too. There were tons of parking spaces, always a plus; in fact if they ever had a parking problem they would know that they had it made. The only issues were that the space as he saw it would take some renovation and a *lot* of cleaning out to be functional, and that the whole property was up for sale. Larry did now vaguely remember seeing a small real estate sign near the property, but lots of things are up for sale, owners testing the waters so to speak, and this was not a big concern for him personally.

Bill was more worried about this, concerned that the Common Good would spend money on renovating and then the place would get sold out from under them: "I know that Dave is committed to the Common Good program but after all he has family and there is a lot of money involved, so how can we be secure? I've been burned before in situations like this."

"We could get a lease that would protect our interests with respect to any improvements, and be binding on any new owners."

"It had better be ironclad." Bill really liked that word, *ironclad*. He used it a lot during that conversation and several others. Somehow it reminded Larry of Al Gore pledging to place Social Security in a lockbox during the 2000 presidential campaign.

Larry just nodded and repeated, "Ironclad man, ironclad, you betcha Lone Ranger." In truth he thought they were getting a bit ahead of themselves—since at that point he had not even seen the space and they had no money with which to pay the rent on this ironclad lease or to make any renovations.

When Larry did get down to the see the place very soon afterwards he was both elated and overwhelmed by what he saw. The large dining room was divided into two portions by a very attractive door wall that could be opened or closed. The western half of the space had a beautiful view of the freshwater pond, the rocky seawall and the ocean beyond it, and the kitchen was behind that section. The other half had a stage at one end and it directly faced a large wooden fence that had been erected by the man whose house was across the road. The western half with the kitchen would be just about an ideal space for the café component of the soup kitchen; all the equipment and furniture that they would need was already there. There were two coolers, albeit with the Pepsi logo on them, and a regular refrigerator to boot. The Wi-Fi from the motel even reached there and would be available for free: what every café needed these days. That all was the elation part.

There was a big very dark room behind the kitchen filled in totally cluttered fashion with tables, trays, dishes, utensils, paper cups, you name it, stuff from the old restaurant. Also the kitchen itself was cluttered to the gills and looked like what it was: an old kitchen that had not been used for too many years. That was the overwhelming part.

Bill talked about opening up a wall between the kitchen and café space to make a pass-through counter, constructing a coffee bar within the café space, and putting some windows in the back room and tearing out the rug to make that into the market space. There was also talk about doing something about the rug in the café space: it was dingy and had a somewhat musty scent. Bill also muttered about what it would take to get licensing approval from the state inspectors as there were some exposed wood surfaces and other things that might be no-no's in the kitchen area, which in fact had not been updated for many years. These things also added to Larry's overwhelmed factor.

Having been set in motion, the wheels kept spinning on multiple tracks at the same time. The pace was accelerating, and it was a very exciting time. It was also a very challenging time—before they could eventually end up calling Seawall their home, the partners had to face many obstacles: the complex lease negotiation, the pricey repairs, and a major disagreement with the board when they least expected it. There would be more than one "that was kind of disappointing" moment in the month to come.

Larry set up another appointment with Peter Roy, and gave him an e-mail heads up to work on the *ironclad* lease. On the day of their appointment, Larry was waiting in a chair in the ground floor ante-room when Peter came downstairs from another meeting. Spying Larry, Peter said: "Well, if it isn't Mother Teresa!" That one moment produced lots of smiles for Larry over the next few days. After the usual initial jocularity they agreed on what was to go into the lease, and, true to his word, Peter had his secretary e-mail it as an attachment to Larry the next day. The ironclad part was there. It was a one-year lease with the Common Good being given the option to renew it for four additional years, one at a time, and the agreement would be binding on heirs or any other new owner(s) of the property. Larry requested one modification: an adjustment to a six-month initial lease term, with four one-year options beyond that; he wanted to be able to have that "out" if need be. If the café/market fell flat and no big seed money investors stepped up, he could in a worst case scenario supplement with his own seed money and make good on a lease for six months, but not beyond that. He ran the lease by Bill, pointing out the ironclad clauses.

After all involved parties had a chance to review the lease, Larry met with Dave and Vickie in the motel office; this was the first time he met Vickie. Dave and Vickie were happy that Bill and Larry were proposing something new for the town. They said that the terms of the lease were fine and they were all for the project but that they did have one concern. "You know, we are getting on in years and if, God forbid, something happened to me, Vickie would not want to run the motel alone." He looked at Vickie at that point who smiled a little ruefully, "and I wouldn't want to run it without her, either. So we want to put something in there that would let us sell without restrictions if something happened to either of us." In effect they wanted some kind of escape clause that in case of serious illness or catastrophe they could break the lease if that was necessary in order to sell. They chatted a while pleasantly about the possible ramifications of all this, and Larry said that he understood their concern and would run it by Bill and the group and get back to them.

Larry drove over to relay this latest news to Bill in person. Bill was very concerned about this development, to say the least. His anxiety antennae were vibrating. "I knew it, I bet there's pressure on Dave to sell the property sooner rather than later, and now the buzz generated by our interest in the property has already increased its value. If we operate a business there, it will further increase its value; so they want to be able to sell and cash in on what we created ... then there's the issue of renovations, we make renovations and the place gets sold out from under us, then that value would be lost, what do we tell our investors? We are talking about a lot of money here." Now Bill was leaning toward possibly looking for another space altogether; but Larry wondered if the situation was really that dire. By the end of their talk, Bill was somewhat mollified but still nervous about the situation; Larry was once again overwhelmed.

Larry left Bill's place to go home and mull it over. When he did, he thought: "James is back in Portland, Eli is about to leave to touch base back home and won't be back till the end of July, so there is no general on the ground; we do not have all that renovation money as no one has stepped up yet as a seed money contributor, and Bill is edging off the deep end with suspicion about the whole Seawall property thing. The peak tourist season is creeping up on us and Bill needs a job, a source of income, which clearly the Common Good cannot provide at this time ..." So he decided to pull the plug. Exercising his own personal form of post-decisional dissonance reduction via press release therapy, he prepared a draft press release stating that The Common Food would just focus on making soup for delivery for this summer out of a kitchen space somewhere, and continue to recruit volunteers and fund-raise to open a café and co-op market when the time was right, but for now those plans were on hold. (Fortunately, as it turned out, the item simply stayed home on Larry's computer and was never released.)

He communicated his decision to Bill and to Eli and he himself drove down to Seawall the next day to relay this in person to Dave. He hung his head and apologized to Dave but said that he, Larry, just had to face the fact that the resources were not there. Dave was bummed, to say the least. He really wanted to support the Common Good program, really wanted to help make it work. He offered to totally back off on his escape clause request if that was an impediment. Meanwhile, Bill was stunned, almost in shock, and said he'd do anything that Larry wanted at this point to get things back on track. Larry took all this in and thought, "Well, maybe there is a way."

But there were still challenges ahead—primarily the hard-to-ignore issue of the repairs that the space would require. After the very first walk-through Larry had been slightly overwhelmed by the work this space might need. As soon as he got home he called to set up an appointment with Mickey Kestner, "the Mick," their friend and a master carpenter, to look the space over and give them some advice and cost estimates. Mickey Kestner was in fact more than a master carpenter; he was a true genius at building, designing, and even inventing things, and held some key patents in the marine processing field in fact. So, bringing in Mickey to consult at this point was the no-brainer of no-brainers, and Larry felt lucky to know him.

Soon after Bill met with Mickey down at Seawall—their plans to open up a wall between the café space and the kitchen, build a really spiffy coffee bar with built-in grinders and brewers and such, cover all the exposed wood space in kitchen area, and maybe put some windows in the potential market area would cost in the neighborhood of ten thousand dollars. You can imagine Larry's reaction when this news came in the midst of the lease fiasco. "That was kind of disappointing" didn't begin to cover it.

But he later contacted Mickey and learned firsthand that at most a few hundred dollars of cosmetic touches were the only ones that Mickey saw as actually *necessary* to make the kitchen licensable, and that the coffee bar, something pretty important to the operation, would be in the neighborhood of one thousand bucks, plumbing included. They would save money because Mickey wanted to try a new technique, a concrete composite that looked like shiny granite but was much cheaper. "Leave it to Mickey," Larry thought admiringly. The other renovations were things that he and Bill had talked about but were not required. So, okay, Larry thought they could get the café up and running, secure the kitchen, and have some kind of token mini-market in the café space for a very modest cost and the whole renovation issue would be finessed for now; no big expense, thus no worry about compensation in case it didn't work out and they moved. Then, he thought, since Dave was so bummed, he could probably make a deal to get some start-up time in the Seawall space for minimal cost, no lease, no rent, and take a shot at it. Under those terms he was willing to press on.

Everyone was relieved and agreed to Larry's new program with a sigh of relief: the Common Good would just pay the estimated utility costs for the place to Dave at least until they were up and running and actually making money there. They could just have Mickey do the coffee bar, Wicked Joe Coffee Roasting Company would give them the coffee brewing apparatus for free to set them up, and Larry and Bill could see what happened.

On to the next challenge: the tourist season was now upon them and Bill needed solid income. After holding off because of his obligations to the Common Good, he finally had to act and landed a job at a new restaurant that Chow Maine was going to open. The owners had decided to open their own sit-down restaurant in the space that Bill and Larry had briefly considered for the Common Good. Bill said he was just going to be chef and would not take on managerial duties—he needed to devote some time to the soup kitchen. But balancing his new job with his soup kitchen and Common Good duties would prove to be a major challenge.

Bill headed down to the kitchen at Seawall to have a closer look. He concluded that minor surface repairs to the space were not going to cut it. He called Larry that evening and reported that he could not really produce soup or cook in that kitchen for the summer. It wasn't set up properly, it would take a lot of work to make it functional, it would be too inconvenient with him working at Chow Maine to have choppers come down to Seawall (since Chow Maine was around the corner from his house he could have stuff simmering and check on it and that would make juggling things easier), and so on. He listed about eighteen cogent reasons why it would not work for him to cook down at Seawall that summer. Larry was tired, and Bill was the chef, and he had Larry convinced at reason three that it would not work for him, but Larry continued to listen patiently to the rest of the homily, put up no argument, and moved on in his head.

When Bill was finished, Larry pressed the little red telephone icon on his cell phone and hung up. Now Larry recalled the old Art Carney line on *The Honeymooners*, spoken to Jackie Gleason: "What a revoltin' development this is!" They had finally secured the space and advertised it, but the chef couldn't cook in it—so how could they operate a café?

Larry created an interim plan B. He did fully understand and was sympathetic to the fact that Bill was torn between doing what he needed to do to make a living and doing what he just loved doing; he realized that Bill was going to have to do a lot of juggling and was going to be a bit frantic about it for a while. Larry would ask general on the ground James to just run a coffee shop with "healthful" baked goods and a simplified breakfast operation for a while—with that and the free Wi-Fi they should attract a bunch of people to the place. This would serve as further recruiting and fund-raising for the co-op and full café operation down the line. He had a vision of a self-serve breakfast operation lined up on the marble counter that was already in the space: hot oatmeal and twelve-grain cereals, granola, wholesome cereal toppings like raisins and nuts and flax seeds and raw brown sugar, a great looking breadbox and self-serve toaster and homemade jams. It would be modeled on the offerings at the Esalen Institute in Big Sur, California—a place Larry loved and had visited that past February. They would call it the *Healthy Hearty Breakfast Bar.* With the demand for soup down in the summer, Bill and the volunteer crew could probably produce enough soup and salads to have at least some product for sale for self-serve or takeout lunch down at Seawall too, eventually. It could even be transported there if it was cooked somewhere else. That was the plan for now.

James agreed to be part of the new plan; he would come up and help get things started up and run the coffee service, breakfast bar, and limited café operation for the summer. When he arrived they took some publicity pictures down at Seawall: James and Janice pretending to be lunching, café style with the ocean view behind them. Larry had been carrying around an image of the café space since April: there would be a cooler with soups and salads and maybe sushi rolls and wraps in it. People would come and purchase things out of it, and then either take these things home or make themselves comfortable at a table; the staff would heat the soup, put the salad or whatever on an attractive plate. Here at Seawall they had all that: the coolers, the plates and utensils, the tables with a spectacular view. The pictures came out beautifully and they quickly put them up on the Web site, and got them printed in a newspaper article about the soup kitchen/co-op finding a home at Seawall—at last.

Meanwhile, they got some fortuitous additional help improving the kitchen space and making it more work-ready. Mike Sanders from down the road (the computer hardware guy) and lobsterman Mike Sawyer (also down the road from Larry) agreed to help Bill and James see what they could do about cleaning up the kitchen. The rainy, windy, foggy June weather at the moment was keeping the lobstermen on shore. With all that muscle power they got a lot done in one afternoon; then James stayed really late and scrubbed a lot of stuff clean. Bill was impressed, his spirits buoyed. He called Larry and said he might be able to cook down there after all!

Just when everything seemed ready to fall into place, at the eleventh hour even more challenges presented themselves. Larry, determined to make this happen, nipped them both in the bud. First, the board meeting that was meant to stamp final approval on the selection of the Seawall location went awry: there were last-minute suggestions to find another location, perhaps a more centrally-located one, and the board wanted to stall on committing to Seawall. Larry was extremely frustrated. He thanked the board members for their lively and useful discussion, but reminded them that their role was merely advisory. He recounted his handy bus analogy, and told them that this bus was going to Seawall and he needed an advisory board to help them make that plan work; he would understand if those who had a different vision chose not to serve on the board at this time. Most did indeed stay on board and support the Seawall location.

They faced one final last-minute challenge: another renter expressed an interest in renting the space (stiff competition for tenants who were essentially moving in for free). Larry immediately made the five-minute drive down the road to the open sea to meet with Dave. Larry was determined to make this work. He liked the vibes at that point. They had a lot of hard-earned momentum from the fund-raiser, the latest news article, and the updated Web site; the kitchen was looking good and the renovations were well in hand; they had a promising contingency plan; and James was on the ground supported by an ever-growing crew of committed volunteers. The feel of the place was great when you sat there. So he decided to go for it, exercise *his* fearless optimism, and commit to the original lease deal through December. After all of these ups and downs, it looked like they were at a place where they could possibly negotiate a lease at Seawall that everyone could be comfortable with. He would be the seed money investor to get them started, and simply hope that the café would bring in enough income to pay rent beyond the first month or so. They shook hands and the deal was done—Seawall would be the Common Good's new home.

11
July:
Hurry Up and Wait for Godot

Now that the Seawall space was secure, it was time to mobilize to get it up and running. Larry and Bill had planned to hold a white-linen "fancy" fund-raiser dinner in late June or early July, which would bring out the moneyed crowd who "summered" on the Island. If you summer or winter somewhere you are affluent, Larry knew. (Funny, though, he had never heard of anyone who "autumned" in Vermont or who was "springing" in Colorado.) Dreaming big as always, Larry imagined a full house, tables full of casually well-dressed folks, elec-

Leanne Nickon. She opened the café every day, and her scrumptious baked goods attracted people and donations to keep the Common Good alive all summer.

tricity in the air; a special guest table for residents of the Ridge Senior Citizen apartments who would bring tears to the eyes of the audience speaking about what Bill's special soups mean to them. Larry would say a few well chosen words and a financial bonanza would result from the evening one way or the other. Being eminently realistic in this case, Bill said that there were neither time nor resources to put such a dinner together at this point, and they still did not have their license to operate the kitchen commercially, a fairly cogent point. So they put the fancy fund-raiser on hold. Instead they focused on a casual opening evening party and fund-raiser, donations in the bowl as usual, and settled on Sunday, July 12, for the target date. There was a lot of work to do before then.

Mickey got going on the coffee bar construction; Bill and James got another work crew together to do more cleaning and to take inventory of bowls and plates and silverware and such. Jenny Cline arrived with the array of decorative pottery bowls, each unique, and they were set out on the café tables, adding considerable panache to the ambience of the place. Jim King, the innkeeper known for his fabulous decorator's eye, came down with Bill one day and discussed possible color schemes and such, how maybe some judicious accent painting of a wall here or there could raise the aesthetic level of the place. Airing out the place and vacuuming seemed to dissipate the musty smell. The rug continued to be a problem: Could it be cleaned? How much would it cost to replace it? Was it worth it? A variant of Mark Twain's famous dictum came to Larry's mind often that summer: "Everyone talks about the rug, but no one ever does anything about it."

Larry began thinking about how to decorate the space for maximum impact and minimum expense. He started with how he envisioned it being used, which in his mind was as a place for hanging out. Larry was a master at hanging out and envisioning hanging out. He was also further inspired by a book that James had shown him: it was called *The Great Good Place*, by Ray Oldenburg. In effect it was a book about how the coffee house or espresso café could become a third place in people's lives in America, the way the pub was a third place in England, or the café a third place in Paris. The first two places were of course work and home. At the third place one could hang out, relax, and have casual social contacts, much more free and easy and flowing than inviting someone to one's home. Such a third place was a very valuable addition to the quality of life, and of course from the beginning Larry and Bill had envisioned the Common Good Café becoming such a third place for the community, especially in the winter when they really needed one. Larry's experience was that when you are in this kind of place and in hang-out mode you often are looking for something to look at, to read or whatever. Voila! It came to him. The walls would be decorated with pictures and text telling the story of the Common Good Co-op and Soup Kitchen. The text would be oversized and mounted on display board like in a museum show. It would tell the whole story: the original Bill soup kitchen statement, the Kemo Sabe moment, the origin of the word *restaurant*, the basic elements of the mission statement, the importance of gathering resources in the summer to sustain the community in the winter. There would also be large, colorful pictures of food being prepared, of people enjoying food, of food all by itself. All of this would help put greenbacks in the donation bowl as well. Once more, Larry got to work producing text for the Common Good, and this time selecting pictures as well.

No one seemed to really understand what Larry had in mind for the wall space, so he turned to his nephew Ben Rothman, who was in fact summering in Maine with Larry and Fran as he had for many years. Ben had graduated with a degree in psychology from the University of California San Diego several years earlier: by his own account his minor in college was Ultimate Frisbee. He had been inspired by Larry's tutelage to take up competitive croquet as a hobby, and was now on the way to establishing himself as the number one player in North America, the Tiger Woods of croquet as it were. He was very smart, energetic, and resourceful and was in fact becoming successful at joining the small cadre of croquet players who earned a living as pros, through running tournaments and clinics and doing private teaching. Ben would be the one to take charge of getting the display boards ready and hanging them. There was a big space over the counter on the wall between the café space and the kitchen. A giant blow up of the logo would grace the center of that space, color photos of food would be on the right, and a huge picture of a smiling Bill in a chef's coat stirring soup in a pot would be on the left. Larry had taken that rare picture of a simultaneously smiling and cooking Bill, and for aesthetic effect had converted it to black and white for blow up and mounting. He went over the display strategy with Ben, who drove to Staples in Bangor, forty-five miles away, for the necessary materials, and installed the displays. They looked terrific.

Larry met with James to go over the start-up plan: in addition to set-ting up for coffee and pastries, James was charged with doing stuff like getting a phone line, getting the electricity in their name, getting a sign made up to hang on the outside that said "Café and Wi-Fi," and so on. James's most critical task at his point was filing the application to get the license from the state to certify the kitchen. How long this would take and whether they would run into any snags was the big question mark in Larry's mind, and everyone else's associated with the project as well. They had easily obtained a permit from the town to operate a business there, but the state license for the kitchen had expired some years ago and that meant a new application to the folks in Augusta. James had stopped at the licensing division of the Maine Department of Health and Human Services on his way up and picked up the ap-plication. He reported that it was straightforward and easy enough to fill out except for one section: since the property was not on the town sewer system they had to file a plan of the septic system, to show it was adequate for the proposed use. It explicitly said that application would not be accepted without such a plan attached.

As it turned out this would be a major snag in moving forward with licensing. Annabelle had never given Dave a plan for the septic system, and they couldn't ask her for one, because sadly she was now deceased. The system was clearly adequate, as it had been put in sometime in the '90s and could support both a restaurant and a motel; but there was nothing to document it. Dave kindly offered to check with the town and with the two companies on the island most likely to have installed the system, but no one of them had any record of doing that job. An-nabelle, in her independent ways, had probably hired someone from off the island. Though it was unlikely that she had filed some kind of plan of the septic system with the state, Larry called them, trying to touch all the bases. The person there said that a search normally took a week to ten days (and additionally, the person who did the searches was on vacation for the next week). It got even more complicated. Reading over the search request document, Larry hit an item that asked for the date the system was installed. Further, in parentheses, it said that if this information was not supplied, no search could be initiated. Talk about the perfect catch-22! This gave Larry a chance to tell this particular little frustrating bureaucratic tidbit to all who enquired about the state of the licensing application over the next week or so.

A solution appeared to Larry, his brain having locked down into problem solving mode sometime back in mid-May or thereabouts. What they needed to do was hire a septic system specialist to file a report and plan for them on what actually existed as far as he could determine. That would be the best anyone could do. But how to find someone qualified, but willing to do a consulting job for $150 instead of installing a system for $10,000? Larry got in touch with Rick Foster, aka "Froggy," a good friend and excellent plumber who put him in touch with a septic consultant that he knew. They made arrangements for the consultant, Al Eggleston, to come down to Seawall the next week. When Al came down and inspected the septic system, he wrote his report and printed it out in his car, right on the spot. James had the report in his hands and would drive it down to Augusta with the rest of the application the very next day. It basically said that as far as Al could determine the system was fine, though there were some components he could not assess and thus not attest to. Larry thought that this would be good enough; he was beginning to sense that the septic report was to some extent a pro forma requirement, and that any good faith effort would pass muster. He turned out to be right on this score—but for now they would have to simply keep waiting.

It was time to shape up the Seawall space for the opening. Before he left on a Fourth of July family retreat, Larry sent out the requisite press release and printed flyers for the opening party and lined up some live music, a jazz trio. Larry had kept up a steady stream of press releases throughout the late spring and early summer, all of which were printed in the *Bar Harbor Times,* and most of which made it into the *Mount Desert Islander,* the other local paper, as well. Larry received only a few frantic phone calls while on family retreat. Bill called Larry on Friday and said that he had gone and cleaned up the café to the best of his ability, that the decor looked great. Bill would be doing the food for the party, an expanded version of his dinner meetings at the house back in April. They had plenty of volunteer sheets, brochures, and mission statements on hand. All was ready for the opening, the day after Larry returned home.

The party was a triumph. Tons of folks showed up once more. They of course now had a built in base of volunteers, their family and friends. Much enthusiasm was expressed; the space was cooed over; the display boards were read assiduously by most if not all. Bill brought an elderly lady over to meet Larry. She had come down to Seawall to thank Bill and Larry. It seems she had recently moved from a senior residence complex in Massachusetts to the Ridge Apartments in Southwest Harbor because her sister told her about the good food that Bill was delivering each week.

They took in over a thousand dollars in donations at the opening party. They opened on a daily basis after that, to publicize the program and take in donations. Since they could not legally sell stuff made in the kitchen in the absence of the state license, they decided to just provide free coffee, Wi-Fi, and pastries from 8 a.m. until noon every day, talk up the program, and have the donation bowl out. They could probably charge for coffee but would probably take in more through donations anyway. James agreed to man the café and provide this coffee service while they were waiting for the license to begin café operations.

The woman who received the application from James and logged it in said that the inspectors were going to be in Machias, way down east in Washington County, for the next few days, and it might be till the end of the next week or the week after that before anyone would get out to Seawall. Lots of folks told Larry that the state had cut back its inspection personnel, and they should prepare to wait a while. Larry felt fine about waiting a couple of weeks if they had to; the seed money he had "invested" would tide them over till then. All of the money in the bowl would go directly to soup production. No overhead, no administrative costs would come from donations; this would be their watchword for the summer.

As they waited for the licensing inspection, Larry kept busy learning the ropes of the nonprofit world, dealing with all kinds of red tape and new challenges. First, some ideological issues surfaced. Bill and Larry both knew that in any program trying to support natural foods and a healthy diet such issues were bound to arise. Bill, who was not thin, would often say: "I know I talk the talk, but I don't walk the walk. I cook natural food, whole grain, low-sodium, low-fat food, but then at night I go and eat a steak with mashed potatoes and butter and gravy and something sinful for desert." He made vegan soups and salads for the soup kitchen but he was neither vegan nor vegetarian. This issue had surfaced early on when Dr. Geoff Knowles showed up at Bill's kitchen door early one morning soon after the soup kitchen was established and wanted to discuss the whole meat issue. Dr. K had at one time been a strict vegetarian, but had since concluded that meat was really a necessary part of one's diet for optimum health, that we had evolved as meat eaters, and that that the trick was not to eliminate meat but to get meat from natural, organic sources. Bill assured him that they were on the same page, that Bill's vegan soup and salad line was just one facet of his menu offerings.

Now the Pepsi cooler became the focus of controversy: Pepsi as a company represented corporate food America, antithetical to a natural food promoting organization, so the Pepsi logo on the side of the cooler was in itself a problem. But hey, the cooler was there, free, and the only coolers they had were Pepsi coolers, one in the kitchen, one in the café space. Larry brought in an extra Japanese screen panel that he had at home and with Velcro covered the side panel of the Pepsi cooler. But adding to this problem was the fact that Dave had suggested to James and Larry that when they ordered bottled drinks that they should order from Pepsi, since the cooler was on loan for free and they did not want to lose it. Larry commented: "Hey, no problem. Pepsi owns some juice companies and we can stock bottled water and juice from the Pepsi supplier." James had faithfully followed Dave's request though, and included soda pop in the order from Pepsi; the soda of course contained refined sugar and caffeine, among other things. Some natural food–type volunteers saw this soda pop and were outraged, scandalized, shocked to the core. They complained to Bill, and Bill in turn complained to Larry and James. Larry got the soda pop removed; James shook his head. Bill and James put together a food policy statement for the Common Good Café, stating that they would have a vegan line of food but would not be exclusively vegetarian, and that they would be as organic, natural, and local as possible.

On a larger front, Larry knew that there were organizational issues to be addressed all along, but in late June they started coming to the fore. Larry's plan was to have a nonprofit co-op market/soup kitchen that was partially supported by a "for-profit" café. He filed papers of incorporation along with Bill for the nonprofit organization first, since that was simpler and cheaper and they needed to establish that first. They filed under the name of the Common Good Soup Kitchen and Co-op. (James had given Larry a heads up back in May that most co-ops were actually run as for-profit organizations, but Larry figured they could be one of the few exceptions.) Then he filed the paperwork for the café to operate as a for-profit entity, simply forming a business association in the name of Common Good Foods and getting an EIN number from the feds for it. He figured everything was in place, but in mid June he received an e-mail message from attorney Peter Roy's secretary informing him that their articles of incorporation were stalled because a co-op can't be a nonprofit in Maine.

Luckily via his son Andy's contacts, he learned that Fred Stocking, of nearby Lamoine, was a really good legal resource for nonprofits, with over twenty years of experience. Lamoine was quite close to Larry's home in Southwest Harbor, just off the island on the edge of Frenchman's Bay. They coordinated an early afternoon appointment in mid-July, and Larry arranged for their friend Janice to hang out with Franny while he went to consult with Fred. Larry enjoyed the ride after leaving Route 3: first through country farmland terrain on Route 203, then through the center of the town of Lamoine (all twenty-seven seconds of it), and finally along inlets that ring the northwest edges of Frenchman's Bay.

Fred, a tall, hale, and hearty man in his late forties to early fifties with a full head of salt-and-pepper hair, greeted him at the door. Fred had prepared a helpful diagram on a whiteboard sitting on an easel in preparation for Larry's visit. He explained that the best way to look at the legal status of a corporation is via what happens to the assets if it is dissolved: "If the organization is dissolved, the assets of a for-profit corporation go to the owners and stock holders, the assets of a co-op go to its members, and the assets of a nonprofit to other nonprofit, charitable organizations, as determined by the board of the organization that is being dissolved. A co-op is by legal definition organized for the benefit of its members, not for the public good: no matter how much public benefit its existence might provide, it cannot be a nonprofit."

He acknowledged Larry's desire for a two income stream plan and pointed out that there is in fact a standard model for doing that which everyone, including the IRS and the State of Maine, understands. "The standard model is for the profit making entity, the regular corporation or business, to be a wholly owned subsidiary of the nonprofit, operated by the nonprofit corporation for its benefit." In Larry's case, then, the café and market would be registered as a regular for-profit corporation, pay taxes and be subject to all laws governing such corporations. It would however be owned by the soup kitchen, which would be a nonprofit corporation, eligible to be tax exempt. All profits of the café and market would go the soup kitchen as the parent company.

The co-op was the odd man out in this picture. It couldn't be a nonprofit since it was for the benefit of its members and it couldn't be the profit-making arm of the nonprofit for the same reason: *its* profits if any would have to be shared with the members, one way or the other. Larry, mindful of the co-op enthusiasm in his town, confirmed with Fred that the market/café could still have member benefits, i.e. discounts of some kind, just like Sam's Club or frequent flyer miles, right? Fred said sure. "Okay," thought Larry, "the co-op members can become Common Good community members, we won't have a co-op but we will still have a member program—it will at least have a co-op feel." He was relieved to be able to think this way.

Fred also advised that instead of filing for federal tax-exempt status, a complex and expensive process, a better strategy for now would be to get a fiscal sponsor, an already tax-exempt 501(c)(3) organization whose purpose was compatible with that of the soup kitchen, through which tax-deductible donations could be passed on to the soup kitchen.

While driving home Larry mulled over the two new items he now had on his plate, fairly major ones. One was to start searching for a fiscal sponsor, and the other was to figure out how tell everyone that there was not going to be a co-op, and also to change their promotional literature accordingly. He began to work on the second item that evening; he called Bill and they agreed on a name change. Henceforth they would be called the Common Good Soup Kitchen Community. He also changed the literature and logo to reflect this, and he set up a meeting with all the volunteers down at Seawall to explain this change and discuss the program generally.

The next day he began to tackle the fiscal sponsorship issue. It turned out to be a long and twisted road. The first stop on the quest for a fiscal sponsor was the Maine Community Foundation, an extremely well-respected organization that was pretty much the gold standard for non-profits and for donors in these here parts. Despite Larry's high hopes, it turned out that the Foundation, as a philanthropy, could not directly dispense funds to a non-exempt organization like the Common Good. They would still need an actual working charitable or municipal entity as a fiscal sponsor. This was certainly kind of disappointing, but by the time Larry got back to the main road after his meeting at the Maine Community Foundation and was cruising by the mall along a stretch of Route 3, he had popped back into pure problem solving mode. It was time for Larry to have a talk with Barbara Campbell.

Barbara Campbell was associated with the Westside Food Pantry, the charitable organization that gave out food vouchers to folks in Southwest Harbor and the neighboring town of Tremont. It was Barbara who had first suggested to Bill that he deliver soup to the seniors at the Ridge Apartments in town. They could be the ideal fiscal sponsor for the Common Good Soup Kitchen. They set up a breakfast meeting for the very next day at Grumpy's, the new breakfast/lunch spot down at the local private marina. Larry learned a lot about their voucher program, and Barbara said that she would be happy to discuss Larry's request for fiscal sponsorship at the next committee meeting, which was coming up soon. Larry left that meeting feeling good; he could see that one way or another there could be co-operative efforts between them and that although it might take a while, the fiscal sponsorship might materialize there. Later, Barbara Campbell reported back that the board had discussed it, but they had questions, and weren't exactly sure how it would work, or what their fiscal responsibilities would be precisely. It would be something new for them. Larry said that he understood, that these things take time and thought and deliberation. Larry hung up and sighed inwardly. "These things do take time," he thought. Next he tried to see if the town itself could become their fiscal sponsor, but that did not pan out either; it never got past an initial discussion with the town manager.

Several days later he got an e-mail from Sarah Pierce, a friend of Annie Dundon, the physician's assistant and a Common Good advisory board member. "Don't know if you are still looking, but Children, Family & Communities of Ellsworth is a 501(c)(3) with a fiscal sponsorship program, you might want to contact us." He sure might.

Larry contacted Karen Hedger, their director, and learned that they had started a Good Ideas program as a component of the organization several years ago to help start-ups like the Common Good. This time it was a lunch meeting at Sips in downtown Southwest Harbor, with the two founders, Karen and Sara Pierce. Larry might not have landed a fiscal sponsor yet, but for an old guy of seventy-plus years he sure had landed a lot of meetings with women. They met, and it was good. They told him about their organization ("We weren't making any money anyway so we figured we might as well reorganize as a nonprofit. It only took about three years and many thousands of dollars.") He told them more about the Common Good program, their current status and their mission. The Good Ideas program would set up an account for them, receive the contributions, send the contributors a tax-receipt letter acknowledging the donation, and forward the receipts to the Common Good program at the end of each month, sooner if the money was sorely needed. There would be no set up fee, a 5 percent administrative fee on contributions and only a 2 percent administrative fee on grants channeled through Good Ideas. No middle man, no board meetings, no delays. Larry said that sounded fine. Karen said she would draw up a letter of agreement and e-mail it to him pronto. She asked if the Seawall space might be available for a retreat that their organization was holding on a weekend a couple of weeks down the road. Larry said that would be fine too. Had he finally found the right road?

Yes! Karen was as good as her word; two days later the letter of agreement arrived as an e-mail attachment. It was succinct and to the point, but captured the essence of what the IRS required from such fiscal agreements, as Larry had learned from the Maine Community Foundation materials and Web site links that he had checked out. He was impressed with how Karen had simplified the process yet maintained its essence; the Common Good pledged to use the money for the appropriate charitable purposes, and Good Ideas pledged to collect and disburse the money appropriately based on the assurances received from the Common Good. All Larry had to do was download and print the agreement letter, sign and return it, and get a signed copy back from Karen. Voila, it was done—they had their fiscal sponsor.

As luck would have it, the very next day a friend of Larry's, Mr. Anonymous, met Larry on the street and said, "You, know, Larry, if you guys had a 501(c)(3) sponsor, I would make a thousand-dollar contribution to the soup kitchen."

"It so happens we do have a sponsor," replied Larry semi-matter-of-factly. If Mr. A was somewhat stunned or even seriously surprised he hid it well, and said, "Great, well in that case, I can make the contribution. Next time we meet up you can give me the particulars, or you can send me an e-mail with the details." Larry said that he could do that very thing. It took a while to get all the particulars down, but eventually the contribution was duly made: the Common Good had their first Paul Newman club member, though he was not requesting a soup created in his name. The very next day after that, as it happened, someone who came to down to the café space at Seawall also wrote a thousand dollar check, so now they had two Paul Newman club members, two donations to funnel through their fiscal sponsor. It could be the beginning of a beautiful friendship. Larry realized he was beginning to actually learn some things about operating in the nonprofit world as well. In ten years or so if he kept going at this rate he might catch up to his youngest son.

The day of the late July volunteer meeting at the Seawall space arrived. It was very well attended: over two dozen folks. Hannah Whalen showed up, much to Larry's delight. By that time their volunteer list, which Larry had copied for distribution at the meeting, numbered close to fifty, though of course some of them were volunteers only on paper thus far. Still, they had come a long way in a short time. Mary McClaud was there for the first time, and had tears in her eyes as she looked around at the space and at all the people that were sitting there with her. "I can't believe that the soup kitchen that started in Bill's kitchen with little donations from my hair salon has blossomed into this ..."

Larry began by explaining what Fred had told him, and outlined the plan going forward: they had already re-filed as the Common Good Soup Kitchen *Community* to become a Maine nonprofit corporation; next they would take the business association one step further and set up a for-profit corporation or LLC, Common Good Foods, that would operate the café and the market once they had the license to operate the kitchen. They would be up and running on the profit side as soon as they could; in the meantime they would keep their presence with the free Wi-Fi and coffee and pastries, which had been drawing in contributions between fifty and one hundred dollars daily at that point. The soup kitchen was beginning to accumulate a little bit of a cushion, mostly from tourists grateful to receive the free Wi-Fi and coffee and supportive of what they read about on the walls of the café space at Seawall.

There was a lively and enthusiastic discussion. There were questions about the soup, how much were they delivering and exactly to whom, and some people had heard that the soup was too spicy whereas others had heard that the soup was too bland. There were questions about recycling and how they could be more "green" and questions about how they might spruce up the space a bit, especially the outside entrance. Of course everyone wanted to know when the café would open for business, when the license would come through. The state licensing people's official word was "Don't call us, we'll call you," and that was all Larry could say. He was hoping that call would come soon.

The discussion turned to fund-raising; if they were to apply for grants they would need more data on number of clients served, area served, how many potential soup clients there really were in the area served, and so on. Larry saw that the grassroots nature of what they were doing was both a strength and a weakness—the personal contacts of people like Joni were getting to people with a need for "soup and soul" for sure, but this was not a systematic way to reach people or to document what they were doing for funding agencies. They needed to beef up that part of the program but still in a grassroots way. They needed ten Jonis. If this could not happen they needed a more systematic plan to recruit clients and delivery people.

The last item on the agenda was publicity. Hannah W. made some very useful suggestions, including having a soup event at Seawall: bringing people down there from the senior residences to enjoy free soup in that space, learn about the program, and take some soup home. Perhaps they could team up with Island Connections, the group that provided transportation via volunteers to seniors and the disabled? This idea hit Larry like a thunderbolt. Of course! So simple, and right under their noses. They had been so focused on the unconventional aspects of their soup kitchen program, which originated by *delivering* soup, that they had overlooked the most obvious thing that they could do at the Seawall space—actually serve soup to people there. The next day he called Chris Keefe of Island Connections and began making plans for a soup event in September. There would be live music at this event, too.

Another jaunt was coming up for Fran and Larry, this one for their oldest grandson's wedding in St. Joseph, a town in the southwest corner of Michigan on the lake of the same name. Just before leaving he met with James, who said that maybe it was time for him to go back to Portland. There was little happening here in terms of the café space, as the state inspection hadn't happened and whenever he called they now gave him the standard "don't call us, the inspector will call you" and reminded him that it could take up to four weeks or longer. The various start-up tasks had been accomplished: phone, electricity, coffee bar, basic supplies and accounts to purchase them, signage, licensing application. That job was done, they did not really need him any more, and he was not comfortable just hanging out and not being able to actually operate the coffee shop as a business. Larry understood, was not totally surprised, thanked James, and the next day headed off for Michigan with a new issue to ponder in addition to all else that he was pondering: who would replace James for the everyday opening of the free Wi-Fi and coffee café?

The wedding was a delight, as the town was charming and all of Larry and Fran's kids were there: Marc, Janet, Peggy, and Andy. Larry thought, "Hmm, I have these things I am pondering about the soup kitchen, especially how to replace James in one way or the other. Why not share all this with the kids and break down that arbitrary self-imposed separation between "work life" and "family life"? It dawned on him that the kids could be a great resource. He had never quite thought of the kids in this light before; he had been proud of them for who they were as people, but now their skills and accomplishments and the experience and wisdom that they must have acquired, each in their own way, also became a source of pride. The family found time to literally have a round table discussion in the catering hall during the reception.

He gave them a brief overview and then came to the James issue and specifically sought their advice, going over the various candidates to replace him. They had some seed money funds still available that they could use to pay a stipend to the person who opened up and made the coffee and hung out every morning to collect contributions while they waited for the state inspector to show up. The kids concurred that some kind of stipend was a good idea if you wanted someone to show up every morning and work. They noted that when you have a volunteer organization that has some kind of paid position, it is politically very tricky. The Common Good needed to advertise the position and go through what was tantamount to a hiring interview process so that all would be transparent in order to avoid hurt feelings among the volunteers. They acknowledged that running a nonprofit could be complicated, that starting one up was sure demanding, and they expressed their admiration for Larry's efforts. His oldest son Marc said that among the various executives, engineers, and so forth that he had taught in project management classes, the best student by far, the one that stood out above all others was in fact a woman that ran a nonprofit. "What kind of nonprofit?" inquired Larry with interest. "A daily soup kitchen," replied Marc. "She is the only paid employee in an organization with three hundred volunteers."

"Karma follows you everywhere," thought Larry. Maybe he should get the e-mail address of that woman?

As it turned out there was only one person with an interest in the café position; the board liked her too and she assumed it immediately. It was Leanne, who had volunteered to chop back in May, and then had further volunteered to bake goods at home and bring them down to Seawall. She agreed to hold the fort, to bake little scones and muffins and brew the coffee and open every morning at eight and be there until twelve. Her scones and muffins were simply scrumptious: light and delicious. And so a new era down at Seawall began, for how long no one knew. At this time Larry also got to work sculpting a briefer, one-page statement about the Common Good to make their vision more accessible. It listed three major goals for the organization: operate the soup program, enhance community spirit, and act as an agribusiness antidote.

So, they had a nice new statement and a nice new plan to run a soup event, but as the summer rolled on with no licensed kitchen, they were not only losing revenue but also losing enthusiasm among the volunteers, who were getting tired of waiting for Godot. Larry called the licensing division of Health and Human Services several more times; he tried to politely get across the message that he knew that they were understaffed, he knew it could be a while, they just needed to know how long a while, could someone tell them where they were in the queue at least, give them an idea of when the inspector might get down there so that they could plan? Sometimes he got the simple robotic rejection of his request for information and sometimes he found someone sympathetic who pledged to call the inspector and have him get back to Larry, but even in the latter case the inspector's call never happened. Larry too was beginning to get restless and apprehensive about the waiting process.

These were trying times for the Common Good program. In addition to the license process being bogged down, Bill was getting more bogged down with his Chow Maine job, and they still did not have enough folks on the ground on a regular basis to tend to things at the facility. They could not just sit there dead in the water; like a shark they had to keep moving. Larry tried to fire up the troops and started brainstorming about a volunteer appreciation party/fund-raiser with food and music for a Saturday night in early August. This would lead serendipitously to even better things down the road: game saving, hail-Mary pass, home run in the bottom of the ninth, three-point shot at the buzzer kind of things. Those things took a while to happen though; what actually happened next was that Larry had a mid-summer meltdown sparked by a seemingly trivial incident.

Bill had been struggling to find time to organize the Seawall kitchen and the soup production and distribution volunteers while working at Chow Maine. He had to juggle a lot, and often would call Larry at the last minute to get volunteers to come down or get something else that was needed because there was no regular schedule now: they were fumbling to put one together. Larry's phone rang one morning during his prime time with Franny, sometime between ten and noon; he ignored it as he was engaged in grooming activity that he did not want to interrupt. When he had time to check the phone a bit later he saw that the phone call had come from the soup kitchen phone and he wondered what was up this time? He checked the voicemail message that had been left and heard Bill, somewhat excited and enthusiastic, telling Larry that the crew was down there prepping to make soup and wondering if Larry had a boom box that he could bring down to Seawall for them to have music to chop by? Larry went boom-boom inside! "He's calling *me* to bring him a #*$%@ boom box? That is my job now? Am I his flunky? Bill knows how over-committed I am. Am I now supposed to limp upstairs, rummage around to find a boom box and interrupt everything I am doing to lug it down to Seawall? This is important? He has the nerve to ask that, expect that of me, to interrupt me for this?!" Larry was livid. Livid was his middle name at that point.

He did not want to interrupt the soup production; he would set up a meeting with Bill for that night or the next morning to tell him what he thought. In the meantime he produced a written letter to Bill on the computer, a diatribe, and then tried to go about his daily routine with Francine as calmly as he could. Eli called in the late afternoon while Larry was walking with Sofia in the blueberry field. Eli was heading back to Maine soon and he wanted to know how things were going. Larry explained his lividness. Eli innocently enquired as to why Larry was so livid about such a small thing and that made Larry even more livid. Eli tried to calm Larry a bit.

Later Larry spoke to Bill on the phone and told him he was pissed and that it was Bill he was pissed off at and they needed to talk. "Can we talk tonight after you get off work or meet tomorrow morning to talk face to face?"

"We could meet tomorrow morning," Bill said, "but I want to know, really need to know now what you are so upset about."

Larry really did not want to have that conversation on the phone, but what the hell, he thought and told him. Bill apologized; for sure he should have called someone else, not Larry. He did not see Larry as a flunky, respected Larry to the max, did not mean any disrespect, just got carried away with the moment. Larry felt a little better, a little less livid, but not that much. He hung up and went about his business. Later Eli called him to say that he, Eli, had talked to Bill and that Bill was very shaken up and very apologetic. Eli told Larry that he thought Bill had in a way wanted to share his good feelings with Larry, that he was excited and proud to have gotten the soup production well organized down at Seawall and called Larry because he wanted to display that to Larry, make him feel good too. "He sure produced the opposite response," muttered Larry.

Larry calmed down enough over the next few days to begin to examine his own response to the boom box request. Why *had* he exploded like that? That question led him to realize for the first time that he had made an implicit bargain with himself: he could do the soup kitchen thing as long as it interfered as little as possible with his caring for and nurturing Francine and taking care of the domestic front generally. Documents on the computer, e-mails, press releases could for the most part be done outside of prime time so to speak. Occasionally there was an important meeting with an attorney or someone that could be planned for in advance, but phone calls during prime time were an annoying and somewhat guilt-producing interruption; they were taking time away from Francine and maintaining the house so they better be important. He resented the interruptions for this reason and this one in its triviality really set him off. He realized that because the bargain was implicit it gnawed away at him emotionally in ways he had not fully recognized. He had not realized the extent of the guilt and self doubt about his whole commitment that he had been carrying around. He vowed to simply ignore phone calls during prime time rather than go around feeling angry and guilty about them. This seemed a more sensible way to go. It was.

Eli got back into town, just in the nick of time. Leanne was holding the fort as far as making coffee and pastries and opening up every morning, but they needed someone else on the ground, attending to all the little details like mouse control, cleanup, faucet fixing, deliveries, bumpy ramps at the entrance, volunteer schedules, you name it. Eli agreed to be that man on the ground, after which he would most likely be heading back to Michigan. They got into a routine: Eli would hang out at the house, keeping an eye on things and being there for Francine, just in case, in the early mornings while Larry walked Sofia, met with people briefly, or did other errand type things. When Larry got home Eli would head down to the soup kitchen/café and check on things, jolly up the visitors, and deal with whatever came up so that it would not interrupt Larry during prime time. Larry was amused to find that when he came back from his early morning rounds Eli was never in the house: he was in fact sitting on a folding chair next to the tailgate of his small SUV, with his propane coffee maker operating, reading or on his iPhone. Eli was so used to living out of his car on fishing trips and such that this was what made him most comfortable. Larry began calling him "the Bedouin," more comfortable in his tent than he could be in any house.

They began to prepare for the August party and fund-raiser and still there was no word from the state inspector. One morning a funny thing happened that seemed to provide nothing more than trivial amusement at the time but ended up actually having an impact on Larry in spite of himself. Larry walked into Sips café and Rick Griffin, the short order cook, saw him enter from behind the stove. "Good morning, Larry," he said. "You know the way people talk about you, you are kind of like the godfather in this town. They call me the mayor, but *you* are the godfather." Larry smiled and was tickled; he certainly had not ever thought about himself in that light before. A few days later Eli came back one evening and said to Larry: "You had better be careful. People are getting too dependent on you. They act like you are the godfather or something, won't make a move without checking it out with you first."

"Not you too!" thought Larry, and again he was tickled. He also realized that godfather or not, he was "waiting for Godot" like everyone else—the summer was almost half over and they still could not really launch their operation without the license from the state.

12

In the Back of the House: Whole Grain Salads

One day a Ridge resident said to me, "Soup is nice, but you can only eat so much soup. You got anything else?" I laughed and said I would see what I could do. I realized after I got home that I could take the same ingredients I had been using in my soups and create whole grain and vegetable salads, such as the recipes below—like making whole grain vegan soups but leaving the water out!

Kasha Varnishkes Salad with Pumpkin Seeds

Kasha Varnishkes is a dish I got attracted to because of my love for buckwheat groats, i.e. kasha. Kasha you have to be gentle with or you will end up with something brown that tastes like what it looks like—dirt. They can be served hot or cold but I decided to make a cold salad out of this dish, adding things like pumpkin seeds, because it just seemed to make sense in terms of taste and texture. So here it is.

Ingredients:
bow tie pasta
buckwheat groats (cooked until
   soft in water like rice with
   a dash of tamari, sea salt,
   ground nutmeg and allspice)

dill, picked but not chopped
salt and pepper to taste
a little white wine vinegar if
   you want, but not a strong
   taste of it

olive oil

scallions, sliced in slivers

roasted pumpkin seeds as topping

Again, the key to this dish is: do not overcook the kasha! When it is just finished cooking (has absorbed all the liquid) turn it out into a bowl and using a rubber spatula, fluff it up to cool, and keep fluffing it periodically until it is at room temperature. Add a little olive oil and rice vinegar on the last fluffing. Add this to the rest of the ingredients as soon as it has cooled. That's it!

Red Rice "Tabbouleh" with Corn

I wanted to make a non-wheat tabbouleh because I really liked my tabbouleh recipe as a vegan grain salad, but the non-wheat vegans were giving me grief. So thank god I picked red rice, first because it worked best and second because I could add corn to it as well. If I was going to piss off everybody in the Middle East by tampering with their traditional recipe, I might as well add something I wanted and liked.

Ingredients:

red rice, cooked al dente

tomato, chopped fresh, lots of it

parsley, finely diced

red onion, small dice, not watery

corn—sweet Maine corn fresh off the cob preferred, of course

lemon juice

sea salt

cayenne and paprika to taste

olive oil—if you want it, but not too much

The key to this dish is to cook the red rice using the Japanese method of preparing sushi rice: cook the rice with the normal 2:1 water to rice ratio and then when the rice is done, turn it out into a big bowl and fluff it with a spatula and fan it to cool it and separate the kernels. You can use a hand fan or an electric fan, or just wave the spatula around in a fanning motion. The idea is to get the heat out quickly. At the same time, i.e., while fanning and fluffing, take your third hand and add:

> rice vinegar
> mirin (rice wine sweetener)
> sea salt, added to taste

Remember that vinegar and salt will always taste stronger once the heat is gone. So be careful—nothing worse than too much vinegar, plus remember that when you mix the rest of the ingredients in you will be adding lemon juice. So be careful with both vinegar and lemon. Use your senses; your tongue is the best cooking measurement tool that you have in the kitchen. Enjoy!

13

August:
Midsummer Problems and Melborps

August was a month of highs and lows, marking both an inspiring rejuvenation of the Common Good project, thanks to a refreshing and energetic new entourage of young volunteers, and the near death of the project as plans to keep it alive during the winter grew confused and then grim. They had a couple of big events coming up in August: a party/fund-raiser for the Common Good, and a catering event for the Bass Harbor Yacht Club. Meanwhile, Bill was still "struggling and juggling" to balance work at Chow Maine with his soup kitchen duties, and Larry was anxious to keep the project moving forward—among other things, they were still waiting for state licensing approval to get the café operation going.

State Representative Elsie Fleming of Mount Desert Island. Her inquiry facilitated the long-awaited licensing inspection just when things looked really dark.

Having scheduled the party date, done the PR, and lined up a jazz trio, Larry thought he'd better line up some food and a serving and cleaning staff as well as do some site preparation. He was able to engage Gillian, Bill's talented teenage daughter, to make a massive platter of veggie sushi rolls, and he got another massive platter of teriyaki chicken on skewers and dumplings from Chow Maine. He had Eli and maybe a couple of other volunteers, but that would not be enough. He then thought of Alex.

Alex was the granddaughter of a dear friend from the world of croquet, Libby Newell. He had met Alex when she was thirteen and a couple of years later had a chance to get to know her well and admire her when she and Larry's young nephew Anton had a summer romance. That had been in the summer of '98, another century. Alex continued to spend most of July in Maine every summer, as a theater arts instructor for the Summer Festival of the Arts, an annual Mount Desert Island program that kept her busy. They had kept in touch only sporadically, but Alex had recently invited Larry to be her friend on Facebook: she was living in Dallas and was a yoga instructor of some repute there, but had plans to spend the entire summer in Maine that year. The picture Alex put up on her Facebook homepage threw Larry off a bit: with her hair trimmed short and dyed jet black it took Larry a while to convince himself that this was really the Alex he knew.

Larry again had the same problem when Alex called out to him one evening at a steel band concert that they were both attending. He regrouped quickly: this beautiful young woman calling his name was Alex, of course! They greeted each other warmly, and Larry and Franny hosted a small dinner party for Alex and their nephew Ben. Larry made daal masala with scallops and fresh mango and sliced crunchy cucumber slices—it was a good dinner and a good time. Now with the fundraiser party coming up, Larry recalled that Alex had expressed interest in the Common Good Soup Kitchen and was finished with SFOA for the year: why not see if she could help out?

She not only could, she said she would bring her friends, Casey and Monica. This was good, thought Larry, very good. Monica was a woman around Alex's age, and Casey was Alex's boyfriend. All three worked hard as volunteers that night. The "entourage," as they were thenceforth dubbed, added a lot to the success to the party with their effort and their enthusiasm for the Common Good project. Jill Freundlich, a stalwart volunteer since early June, came and worked hard and brought her husband Bob to a Common Good event for the first time. Jill and Bob became solid core volunteers that they could count on from then on all through the early fall. Their faithful efforts buoyed Larry's spirits. The party/fund-raiser was a success: in excess of seven hundred dollars was raised. Alex again expressed an interest in volunteering for the Common Good for whatever was needed while she was up in Maine.

Bill was really impressed with the energy that came from the young entourage team. He was still juggling, trying to find a way to get the shopping and chopping and cooking done to keep producing soup while having another full time job that had turned out to be more physically and mentally demanding than he had anticipated. Many of the choppers who had helped out in the winter and spring were themselves overworked with summer employment and/or family visits. Bill hit upon youthful energy as the possible answer: "We need to get more young people involved," he said to Larry the day after the party. "Can't we get some interns from the College of the Atlantic? They are big into the environment and whole, organic foods."

COA was a small liberal arts college in Bar Harbor that had only one major, Environmental Studies and Human Ecology. They owned and operated the Beech Hill farm, an experimental organic food growing program ten minutes from Southwest Harbor. Their own students did internships there and they had a farm stand on the site that was open from June through October. Paul Newman's daughter Nell had graduated from the College of the Atlantic, which helped put it on the map in its early years. Many islanders had fond memories and favorite stories of meeting Newman and Joanne Woodward when mom and pop came up to visit their daughter; they were known for their good will and graciousness to all those around them.

As far as getting an intern for the Common Good program, an assistant for Bill that he desperately needed, Larry was not sure if they would get any bites from COA students since it was summer. But he went to the COA Web site and got the e-mail address for student employment, sent them an e-mail briefly describing their program and their need for interns to help out, and included their Web site address. The very next day he received an e-mail from Fiona Hunter, a student who had grown up on a small farm in mid-coast Maine, worked at the

Beach Hill farm stand, and was very interested in getting involved in a program that aligned so well with her food philosophy.

The mission statement, which had been posted on the Web site, was still working its magic, it appeared. Fiona came aboard and helped primarily to get the shopping done and to buoy Bill's spirits. She also was a key link to the Beech Hill organic farm, from which they both purchased food and received food donations, produce that could make great soup but that was surplus or in some way visually compromised to where it could not be sold at the farm stand. Larry had also hoped that Fiona could set up a small organic produce stand for them down at Seawall, so that the market part of their mission could at least have a token start, but the summer ended and she was back to classes pretty much full time before this could get off the ground. That was kind of disappointing to Larry, but all in all though, it was another example of the right person turning up at the right time to keep the program viable and moving forward.

Now it was moving on towards mid-August and still they were waiting for the licensing inspector. Larry knew that he needed to move the pieces into place for when the inspection happened and they got to open the café for business. They had to continue to be proactive, be ready to seize the moment when it happened. He decided to finally do something besides talk about the rug: after ruling out the possibility of replacing the rug, he arranged for his nephew Ben to rent a rug cleaner from the local hardware store and do a test patch, to see how it came out. It came out great, so that looked like the rug plan.

Larry also knew they needed at least one more refrigerated display case to sell food out of when the café opened, and they needed a freezer. There was a possible source: Laila Dekkaki, a friend of Bill's, had run a small takeout café that was now closed, and she had a bunch of leftover equipment, including display cases and a freezer, that was in storage and that she was now trying to sell. Larry played phone tag with Laila for a while and eventually they caught up to each other and worked out a deal: Laila could store her stuff for free, the soup kitchen could use her freezer, and the Common Good Café would buy one display cooler, making time payments. Larry asked Eli to meet up with Laila and her crew one weekend to help them figure out where it should all go.

"What is this about?" Eli asked Larry, "who is this Laila person? Am I supposed to help move her stuff? I am not going to do that."

Larry smiled, highly amused. "It's Laila, you'll see. I cut a deal with her. She is bringing her own crew, you just have to be there to make sure the freezer and display case get in the right place and help guide them as to where to stow the other stuff."

"But … but … but …" Eli began to sputter. Larry told him to relax, it was Laila, he would see.

When the day came, Eli in fact became one of the crew and helped stow all the stuff away, voluntarily. He reported to Larry: "Holy cow, when I met Laila I was almost struck dumb, I could not say anything intelligent, I would have done anything she asked me to." Laila was in fact a tall woman with dark hair and big dark eyes who was beautiful in a totally magnetic and totally arresting way. Larry just smiled and said. "I told you. It was Laila." Two more pieces were in place.

By this point they had been waiting for an inspection to be scheduled for four weeks. They needed to take some action, but what action and whom to contact? Then Larry thought of Elsie Flemings, the Maine State House Representative for Mount Desert Island. She had attended one of the early dinners for organizing the Common Good program and Larry had met with her back in the spring for a follow-up session. Larry called her and explained the situation and she instantly understood the need to use diplomacy, not a heavy hand. Later that same day Elsie called Larry back and said that she had reached the inspector, that he was apologetic, and that he would surely get to them by the beginning of the following week. The next day Elsie called back and said that the inspector called her again and that he would be getting there by the end of *that* week, Thursday or Friday.

Larry took Franny up to Bangor in the early afternoon on Tuesday; they had an appointment at the cardiologist to do one of the periodic checks on her pacemaker. When they came out of the office into the

August sun at around 3 p.m. Larry turned his cell phone back on and found a voicemail message: it was in fact the inspector saying he was on his way down to Seawall to do the inspection and would be there at 2:30 or so. Of course this would finally happen when he was forty-five miles away! A few frantic phone calls later he found that Bill had been contacted by Dave at the motel and had met the inspector and that the inspection had taken place—they had passed, and were good to go! That night, Tuesday August 18, Larry sent out an e-mail thanking all the volunteers for their efforts and patience, thanking Elsie Flemings for her help, and informing all that the inspector had arrived and that at long last they had their license to operate. He titled it "Jubilation."

As it happened there had already been a volunteer meeting scheduled for late that week. There were slightly fewer than twenty volunteers in attendance, a good turnout considering that folks were maxed out with family commitments, and some, like Jennie Cline were only weeks away from leaving their summer abodes. The jubilation memo must have had a mobilizing effect. Larry realized though that what had been gnawing at him at the edges was getting closer to occurring: they would lose a lot of their volunteers at the end of the tourist season.

There was a lively discussion among those present. Larry outlined the plan for what he was then calling Senior Day, bringing folks down to Seawall for soup and music some Friday in September, and the plans for getting ready to actually open the café as a business. Everything seemed upbeat; certainly they had made lots of progress.

But even amidst this progress and jubilation, Larry was thinking, what next? It might have come too late. He did not see where the resources would come from to actually get a café operation up and running, and if they did it would only be running for a short time, until Columbus Day at the latest, as the tourist crowds were about to dwindle sharply after Labor Day and disappear completely when the leaves fell off the trees in mid-October. Also, Bill had limited time available: it was a strain on him just to make soup for delivery to the Ridge Apartments and Joni's clients each week. Leanne was going away on a trip in early September and was ready to shed the shackles of opening up every morning in any case. Arnold had time only to be a contributing chef and sous-chef; he could not take over regular food production, even if they had someone to manage the store so to speak. Eli was going back to Michigan at the end of August, so they were losing their man on the ground. Contributions came in steadily, but they hadn't been able to cash in on the peak of the tourist season to amass a cushion.

It was time to face the facts. After the volunteer meeting Larry called for a meeting with Eli and Bill, an early Saturday morning confab around Eli's coffee pot in Larry's backyard driveway. He told them both that there simply was not enough money to even think of running a café/market through the winter at Seawall; rent and heat and electricity alone would eat up every penny before the winter even began to turn around. Bill was a bit stunned, Eli not surprised but at a loss: "What will we do? What will we tell people? What will we tell Dave?"

Larry said that there was some seed money left and that if they could actually figure a way to bring in at least some income from food sales they could operate at least a limited café operation through September and maybe into October, and in any event that he would make sure they fulfill the terms of the lease and pay Dave rent through December, one way or the other. Of course Dave would be bummed, everyone would be bummed, Larry was bummed, but that was the reality.

Larry was not ready to throw in the towel, his mind buzzing with ways to make it work, but he also knew they needed a face-saving back up plan if they really had reached the end of the line for now, would have to shut down the Seawall operation. The meeting broke up, the three musketeers as it were went their own separate ways: Bill to mull things over and prepare to work at Chow Maine that night, Eli to try and mellow out in the woods, Larry back to the house and later ultimately to his computer and cell phone to confront this new phase head on and figure out what to do next. He knew that Bill was very dispirited and that concerned him as much or more than anything else in the situation. What to do here? Were there any other rabbits to be pulled out of the hat?

Now the question for Larry was to find a way to actually open the café, at least launch it for the fall, see his healthy hearty breakfast bar come to life, and have a place for the faithful to rally round in the early fall. He thought of Alex—maybe she would be willing to stay in Maine longer, enjoy the color season and run the café? He reached her by phone on the first try. Alex was receptive, she would think it over seriously, she would love to stay longer and would love to work for the soup kitchen, but there were a couple of issues. One, she had to move out of the house they were currently in at the end of August, so would have to find an abode to rent for two months, and two, she was scheduled to go to Denver for ten days in mid-September for a yoga workshop. She would see what she could do and get back to Larry.

Larry could see without being told that Eli and was now eager to return to Michigan. So with Bill overcommitted this week and bummed out, and Eli ready to head out of town, Larry knew that for now he was the lone musketeer, that Tonto would have to figure it all out and take action without relying on the masked man or anyone else. Also he had about a day to figure it out, because if they were to move forward to the next phase there had to be a press release in the upcoming week's papers and that would have to be sent out no later than early Monday morning. This was it: a decision had to be made now, and he had to make it.

If they proceeded to move ahead, they had only a week to get ready to open for actual business, which meant not only PR and personnel, of course, but also setting up to serve food and putting things in place in the space. Many things had to be done: the breakfast bar had to be set up, a cash register of some kind had to be procured, and a way of tracking sales, menus, pricing, etc. had to be put in place. Complicating things further was the fact that this Friday was the long-awaited catering event for which they would have to gear up: dinner for sixty at the Bass Harbor Yacht Club annual meeting. The plan was to prepare food at Seawall and bring it to the site; it would take some mobilization and a lot of time and effort. Eli was busy helping Bill with the catering gig, and they had even suspended soup production for a week or two to allow for the catering and the transition to the café operation. As it turned out, their first catering gig was a culinary success; people raved about the presentation and the seafood chowder was pronounced divine. Monetarily though, after paying for the labor and the food, they just covered expenses on the catering fee; it was true that some people got a little extra income and they did not lose anything and they had made a good impression. Still, Larry saw the catering gig as sucking up a lot of energy from what ought to be their main focus at that point, getting the café up and running.

Not being able to count on Bill for food production because his time and energy was limited and his spirit was down, they would have to scratch around for product. They might have to come up with some funds to procure food prep help and café management help. If Larry sent out a press release about opening the café and made the commitment he had better be prepared just in case to come up with some additional seed money, a couple of thousand perhaps, for what might turn out to be a swan song, four to six weeks of operation. Was this worth it? Larry had a bit of a restless night.

In the morning he thought some more while walking in the blueberry fields with Sofia. Not only would he have to figure out how make it work all this week without any real help, he would have to make that day's decision totally on his own as well, as Bill would most likely be in his Sunday cave not answering his phone and Eli would be in the woods preparing his head to return to Michigan. Sure enough, neither returned his phone calls any time that morning. This was it; it would surely take optimism to commit to going ahead right here and now, but that decision had to be made here and now. He simply decided to go for it and hope that things would fall into place. It was more fear*ful* than fear*less*, if truth be told, but it was optimism. He wanted to see that breakfast bar in operation, he wanted to hold that September soup event, a big chunk of the mission statement actually embodied, and he wanted to let people experience what a community event at Seawall could be like. This would be accomplishment enough, whatever happened down the road.

If you take a cruise around the world, you expend a lot of resources and then it is over; you come home having lived it, and that's it. One way or the other, this would be his world cruise. He also made another decision on that walk, one he had been toying with. He would get the soup kitchen logo tattooed on his arm; he really loved that logo, he had never had a tattoo, and now he would be able to look at it always, display it proudly, and smile whenever he did so.

It was early afternoon of that same fateful day; he and Franny were back from a late Sunday breakfast. Larry began to glance through *The Boston Globe*, which had been delivered to the house. The front page of the Ideas section caught his eye, an article entitled "Happiness: A Buyer's Guide." The gist of the article was that money *can* buy happiness after all. The essentially zero correlation between money and happiness once you get above the basic survival level is primarily due to people spending money the wrong way; they think that amassing things will produce happiness, but what produces happiness is spending money on more ineffable, ephemeral things, like unique travel experiences, special family gatherings, and helping others. There was lots of data to back this up. What a great thing to read to justify his decision, what great timing.

Later that day Alex called—she would do it! Actually, *they* would do it, the whole entourage. It was Monica who put it over the top; she would go back to NYC that week as she had planned, but now not to move back there but instead to move out of her apartment and come back to Maine and work for the Common Good Café in the fall. Alex's Denver trip would be no problem now. Monica had saved the day; again he could not help feeling love for someone he had really not even met. Casey too, who was working nights at McKays Public House, would help out both by managing on some days and doing spruce up and fix up work as well, like scraping and painting the side of the front entrance, something it needed badly. So, at that fund-raiser party that night earlier in the month the entourage had not only scurried around clearing plates and such, they had read the story on the walls, they had picked up on the vibes from the other volunteers, and they had taken the mission statement home and read it—they were ready to help make this work just when they were really needed.

The truth is that without the entourage all of Larry's optimism and his efforts would most likely have gone for naught. They could not have pulled it off without them; three rabbits appeared out of the hat this time and just when it seemed that the game was up. Larry vowed to find them some kind of stipend to help defray their expenses. The big thing that they needed was a place to stay though.

Larry started off bright and early Monday morning getting out the necessary press releases and placing ads for the café opening. He had no regrets about his decision to proceed, but despite the really glorious summer weather and the optimistic support of the entourage, that week in late August turned into his personal winter of discontent. It required lots of work on the ground to prepare for the café opening, and this was the one thing that was most difficult for Larry to do because of other commitments. Man-on-the-ground Eli had only very limited time to help, and Bill of course had no time and was still disgruntled as well. Bill thought that Larry was essentially wrong to just keep going, that it was time cut their losses and run. Larry felt that now it was Bill of all people that was telling Paul Newman that he could not put fresh ingredients in a salad dressing bottle! He wasn't buying the negativism and it made him angry, but not angry enough to distract him—only angry enough to increase his resolve.

The breakfast bar could be set up easily enough: Larry ordered some 8-quart slow cookers to hold the hot cereals, and he already had a spiffy heavy duty toaster in place and custom built oversized breadbox, courtesy of Mickey Kestner. Lunch food was a different problem; they had some good soup in the freezer, and maybe the management crew could put together some healthy salads or wraps, or maybe there would be surplus food from the catering job to tide them over for a while. He pressed on, vigorous despite his discontent, focusing on what had to be done.

Eli built a really sturdy wooden sandwich board sign for them that could be put out in the parking lot near the edge of the road to advertise the café opening. He also got Eli to make sure that there was an adequate power strip installed in the vicinity of the breakfast bar, and made sure that Leanne would bake some of her goodies for next week before she left town for a while. He would see that the café part of the program at least got *launched*, that it opened for business at 8 a.m. on the following Monday, August 31.

A mid-week problem surfaced, but turned into a nice little *melborp* by the end of the week. *Melborp* was one of Larry's favorite words and concepts; it had been conveyed to him years ago in Detroit by Jay Robinson, an auto worker, poet, and philosopher. Jay said that he always tried to change a problem into a melborp—"problem" spelled backwards, thus the opposite of a problem. In seeing a problem as a challenge and solving it you often end up with something better than if the problem had never surfaced in the first place. It was amazing how often this applied once he had the concept, Larry had found. This week's problem turned melborp: the place in Bar Harbor that Alex, Monica, and Casey were going to rent for September and October suddenly became unavailable when the owner had a change of heart about the deal they had just made. Problem: entourage has no place to live. Larry got an all points e-mail out to the Common Good community looking for help. Ann Waldron, who lived down the road from Larry on the shore, phoned early the next morning to say that the modest but still very lovely house with a quite spectacular view next door to her might be available for the fall, and gave Larry the contact information, which he passed on to Alex. It all worked out—the entourage ended up ensconced in really great digs with a great view just down the road from Larry and five minutes from Seawall instead of twenty-five minutes away. This melborp not only worked out well for the entourage, it lifted Larry's spirits considerably. So, this time it was Ann Waldron who saved the day; he sent her a heartfelt thank-you note. Yet again, the right person just appeared at the right time to provide what was needed for the Common Good.

With Eli gone and Bill exhausted from the dual effort of the catering gig and working at Chow Maine, Larry had to delegate himself as the man on the ground to put the final touches together to open that Monday. He went down to Seawall to set up the slow cooker Crock-Pots he had purchased for the breakfast bar. There he learned that another caterer had bestowed six free Crock-Pots on the soup kitchen, surplus hardware from a catering gig in Northeast Harbor. The free ones were only 4-quart capacity though, so they would supplement but not replace the 8-quart sized ones that Larry had purchased. A soup kitchen can never have too many Crock-Pots, Larry rationalized. He got nephew Ben to help him work out the menu and pricing for the breakfast bar and the soup and salad lunch, and to create convenient pre-printed tally sheets to track sales. They were going low tech. Larry rummaged around on Friday night and found a nice rectangular tin box on a dresser upstairs that could be their cash drawer. He found some weather stripping with peel-and-stick tape on it and created cash slots on the bottom of the box; an upper shelf could hold the coins. He went to the local bank and obtained a hundred dollars in cash and coins to stash the box with change for the opening. He created a sign via computer that said: "Cash only please. We are temporarily unable to process credit cards for the remainder of this century." He set up a table for the cash box to sit on and posted the sign on the wall behind it. He created another sign to Velcro to the sandwich board, advertising free Wi-Fi, a healthy hearty breakfast bar, and soup and salad lunch at the café.

He realized that the manager of the day was going to be alone down at Seawall, difficult if it really got busy, and so created the Common Good ambassador program via yet another e-mail to the volunteer group: he asked volunteers to sign up for two-hour stints to be present at the café during open hours to help out the on-site manager, mostly by guiding the guests, telling them about the program, and being ambassadors for the Common Good. He received a pretty good quick response and most of two-hour slots were filled, at least for the first week. On Sunday all they really needed to be up and running was the food for the breakfast bar; there was salad and soup left over from the catering gig to get them started for lunch sales.

Late that fateful summer afternoon, Larry put Franny and the dog in the car and drove the twenty miles to Ellsworth. Sofia had to be walked, which he could do on the nice walking path grounds of the nearby

Woodlawn Museum there. After that Larry could do the shopping and then take Franny out to dinner. He bought the organic oatmeal, twelve-grain cereal, breads, raisins, flax seed, dried cranberries, brown sugar and nuts for cereal toppings, plus milk, soy milk, local jam and local butter supplies. His hip was hurting that day and he was limping around a bit while doing this, which only intensified his ironic inward smile about supposedly *not* being the man on the ground. It seemed fitting too that he had Sofia and Francine with him while carrying out this crucial ground operation. The former enjoyed her walk and the latter her dinner with Larry at their favorite little Japanese restaurant, Green Tea. It was dark by the time he got everything down to Seawall, but they were now ready to open. He planned to meet Alex down there to go over everything one more time the next morning and then they would be rolling. *Que sera, sera.* Larry was ready for his September Song.

14
Sweet September Song

Alex Newell, Casey Cave, and Monica Johnson. They stepped up at the last minute to open the café for business and run it in the fall.

Common Good Café Menu
Healthy, Hearty Breakfast Bar

All you care to eat - $6.99 + tax
Includes coffee and *all* items below

Individual items   *Stand alone price*

Granola or cold cereal—bowl	$3.50
Oatmeal or 10-grain hot cereal —bowl	$3.50

(All cereals include raisins,
  nuts, brown sugar, etc.
  as toppings.)	

Cup of any cereal	$2.10
Whole grain toast w/ preserves -Per slice-	$0.70
Hi-protein hard-boiled egg	$0.70
Mini-muffin	$0.70
Our own baked pastry	$1.17
Deluxe pastry	$2.10
Premium orange juice	$1.40
Tall glass of milk	$1.40

Lunch/take out

Hot Soup

Bowl	$3.50
Cup	$2.10

Daily lunch specials
$7.99 (tax included)

Soups and salads
to go in cooler

Organic fruits
and veggies

Special items
priced as marked

Free Coffee, Tea, Wi-Fi Connection, and Fearless Optimism in a Bowl
provided as a courtesy of the Common Good Soup Kitchen.

122

The first day of operation, the café took in seventeen dollars in sales. There was close to sixty dollars in the donation bowl though, fairly typical for the daily take before they became a café operation. Larry was ready to accept the café operation simply as a noble experiment for the month. The second day receipts climbed to eighty dollars and kept climbing a bit every day, albeit slowly. The donations were holding steady as well. His optimism meter began to switch from fearful to guarded. Larry went to the bank and got a second zippered bag for receipts, and the manager of the day started making daily deposits into the café account, while Larry took care of soup kitchen account. There might be enough income from the café to significantly defray expenses, keep the place open daily into October while maintaining their policy of not touching any of the soup kitchen donation money for the café or overhead, and saving it all for winter soup. The word was getting around and the entourage crew was emitting great positive energy, really impressing the volunteers that stopped by. Larry was being praised for finding such wonderful people. Monica was already back and had thrown herself wholeheartedly into the project. As it happened Larry's nephew Anton called him from Belgium that week. Yes, the same Anton who had been teenaged Alex's boyfriend, now a young European filmmaker. He asked Larry how the soup kitchen was going, as Larry had sent him an e-mail or two about it earlier in the summer. Larry told him about Alex and the entourage now managing the café, working for the Common Good.

"So," said Anton, "you started a soup kitchen and now you are surrounded by beautiful women."

"That about sums it up," chuckled Larry.

They picked a date for the Senior Day: free soup with live music at the café on Friday, September 25. They wanted to get Island Connections on board with it to provide PR and rides for folks if necessary. Larry was bemused by his phone conversation with the director, Chris Keefe. When Larry suggested the twenty-fifth as a date, Chris said, "Okay that looks good, we can meet on the twenty-fifth to discuss the event." Larry had to clarify that the plan was for the event to actually *occur* on September 25, that they were in fact discussing it on the phone right there and then. Chris did come on board, and became an ardent supporter of their program. While he was trying to brainstorm potential musical acts for the event, it hit Larry like a lightening bolt—Frank Sinatra! "Soup with Sinatra," it had a great ring to it, and what could be better for that generation, pretty much his generation. No, he hadn't gone completely loony, he knew that Sinatra was deceased and thus not available—it was a Frank Sinatra impersonator he had in mind. He recalled now that a guy named Don Gooding had done two shows at Sips earlier in the summer channeling Frank Sinatra, and apparently he was great. He was local, lived over near Somesville. Larry tracked him down and Don agreed to perform for a fund-raising event.

Press releases were readied. Those on the Common Good e-mail list, now swelled to over 150 lucky souls, were informed. Flyers were printed and dispatched to the volunteer crew and the entourage team to be plastered everywhere, "and I mean *everywhere*," Larry would add for emphasis. Maybe the godfather thing was getting to him after all. One of the volunteers, Diane Vreeland, was especially diligent in getting the word out; she also volunteered for Island Connections and knew the ropes and where the senior residence apartment complexes were all over the island.

With the Soup with Sinatra event, one piece of the mission statement—using the space as a hub for the community in bringing people together—would be manifested.

Another piece from the mission statement was also put in place: through volunteer Marsha Lyons, a talk on nutrition by Dr. Geoff Knowles was scheduled for September.

Over thirty people showed up for Dr. Knowles's talk; it was well publicized via press releases and flyers. For Larry it was a historic occasion, the first visible concrete plank in the education platform of their mission. He also enjoyed the talk, which reviewed the basics of nutrition, the nature and functions of fats, simple and complex carbohydrates, and proteins. Dr. K made the point that the low-fat food craze, in part fostered by government nutritional guidelines, had been detrimental because it had in fact greatly increased carbohydrate consumption and obesity levels. He said that there were many who now challenged a lot of the conclusions that had been made by the mainstream health community about the bad effects of cholesterol and that he saw a lot of validity to their arguments, that the bad cholesterol argument had been swallowed hook line and sinker without adequate scrutiny. He made the cogent point that you cannot consider food use in isolation, that the use of any given food had to be seen as part of a cultural matrix, a food tradition as it were. Food traditions such as the Mediterranean, French, and Japanese diets evolved over many centuries, micro-adjustments accruing to produce a functional result in terms of health of the population. Our shotgun, faddish, so-called "scientific" approach to food was throwing this accumulated knowledge out the window: no wonder it wasn't working. A lively discussion followed the talk, and lunch business was brisk that day, as many stayed to eat after the talk. The education program was off to a good start. They scheduled a second talk for a Thursday in early October, again just before lunch.

Larry realized that the mission statement itself had become a kind of Bible or Holy Grail or "mandatory mandate" for him personally. The synergistic program that they had envisioned had to have all of its pieces in play to be fully realized, and he was constantly scheming and scanning for opportunities to get the next piece in place. Every piece that they could actually get down, that they could see manifested in reality and not just on paper, was in itself deeply satisfying to him. Alex had also offered a yoga class, which was not only a nice thing in itself but also fit into the overall goal of making the Common Good a community resource and helping to promote a healthy lifestyle. If they had to shut down for the winter, at least they would have been able to show what could be done if the resources were there.

Meanwhile there was the need to solidify winter plans before very long, and talk to Dave and get the word out to the community as well. They were operating in a community fishbowl of their own making and everyone would want to know what the winter plan was. Paramount of course, he still had to see what was what with Bill, see to what extent he wanted to get on board for this new phase, where his body and mind were at after a week or so of sabbatical from the soup kitchen. Near the end of the week he got in touch with Bill and they agreed to meet on the following Tuesday morning, the day after Labor Day.

In preparation for the meeting with Bill, Larry tried to quell his lingering discontent over the negativity of the last week in August. He knew that Bill was under great stress and was torn between Chow Maine and the soup kitchen and the juggling was wearing him down, as were the constant questions that people asked him about the soup kitchen and its future. If it really had no future, maybe better to throw in the towel now? Bill had certainly been leaning that way in his thinking. Further, Larry also surmised that Bill's negativity about proceeding with the café opening could in part be based on his wanting to protect Larry: he thought it was not going to work and did not want to see Larry put more resources into it than he already had, and thus would remain opposed to it. This was a misguided attempt to be sure, from Larry's point of view, but still Larry understood and respected it. So, he drove over to Bill's with an open heart, as they say. He had no inkling of the fact that things were to be shaken up totally yet again. He roused Bill and as Bill came sleepily down the stairs Larry expressed his hope that Bill would be able to get some needed rest. Bill said, not without irony, but very calmly, that he would probably be able to get a lot of rest now, because he had been informed yesterday when he went into work that he had been laid off.

Larry was thunderstruck. He sat in the living room and listened while Bill told his tale. Bill had known that this was ultimately coming, that they would have to cut back on expenses, but thought he was secure at least through the mid-fall—this was a shock. It was a particularly bitter pill to swallow because Bill had ended up being more than a chef—he had organized both the menu and the whole place into a functioning, attractive restaurant, had gone all out and had done his best to draw people to it. All things considered, Bill was as philosophical as one could be at that point. He knew that his employers had to look at the bottom line. He also took this as a wake up call: "Maybe it's time for me to get out of town. The fishbowl here is too confining personally and whatever job opportunities there were around here, even those are drying up in this economy. It might be time to move on; sometimes you need a kick in the butt to show you what you have to do." He seemed to be seriously considering seeking employment away from the island, or even away from Maine for now, but Larry knew that such a step takes much soul searching and that this could easily change over time. Larry just continued to listen, letting Bill pour out his thoughts and feelings.

They eventually got to the soup kitchen. Bill *did* feel concerned for Larry, regretted that they would have to shut down Seawall for winter after all of Larry's efforts, all he had invested of himself in the project. Larry explained as calmly and as soothingly as possible his world cruise perspective: he explained that he needed Bill's blessing and help with this for the next month or so, and said that he would really feel cheated if they did not get to live out the next part of the mission statement, even if it was only for a short time. If the mission were aborted now, prematurely, Larry would really be bummed out.

This did seem to be what Bill needed to hear at that point. He understood and would do what he could. He would most certainly cook for the Soup with Sinatra event, the most critical thing that was needed. They went on to talk about the winter plans; Bill was asked about this topic in town daily, bombarded even more than Larry. He proposed that when they had to shut down at Seawall they donate the soup kitchen funds to the Westside Pantry. After all, they would be feeding hungry folks in the winter through their voucher program, and that was what the Common Good was all about, ultimately. "Maybe that is the best thing that we can do at this point," summed up Bill. Bill's plan was honorable, but there was a part of Larry that was saying to himself that he was not quite ready for an honorable death for the Common Good Soup Kitchen, not quite ready to fall on his sword, for in effect this is what Bill's plan would mean. Maybe he could still find a way for the Common Good to run at least part of its program in the winter.

After this talk, which had been illuminating and healing for both of them, Bill regrouped and began checking out what was happening down at the Common Good Café. He was impressed by the positive energy and energized by the dedication of Alex, Casey, and Monica. He rearranged the coolers for a more appealing display, and by the end of the week he started coming down and cooking. Just making it up as he went along, using what was available because it had been donated or was locally abundant or somehow just happened to strike his fancy as he cruised the local supermarket, he began putting out an amazing array of food for lunch each day. There ended up being over fifty different items in about a ten-day period! Larry recognized that something extraordinary was going on food-wise, and asked Monica to jot down the food that was prepared pretty much off the cuff every day, a job she executed faithfully. Larry had known how talented Bill was, but this level and variety of production "off the cuff" as it were was truly amazing. He had an indelible image of being at the café late one morning and popping his head into the kitchen. There was Bill with all six burners going—pots simmering or pans sautéing, plus the grill going full blast with thick zucchini slices—and some kind of rasta music on the boom box. Bill was totally in the zone. He had become, as Arnold described it, "a food-producing tornado on feet." (Later Bill described this as "playing the piano," what chefs call it when all burners are on and they are going all out.) This is the list that Monica compiled:

> poached squash and spinach puree
> stuffed focaccia sandwich
> baked beans
> barley corn cashew salad
> roasted turkey
> tofu and squash in lobster miso seaweed broth soup
> minestrone soup
> butternut squash puree soup
> coleslaw
> bulgur carrot mint salad

white bean and kale soup
bow tie pasta salad
hummus veggie wraps
vegan potato salad
rigatoni with grilled veggies
whole wheat pasta with basil pesto
eggplant and garlic puree topping for soups
seafood chowder
broccoli and pepper stir fry
blueberry sauce for hot cereals and muffins
grilled zucchini sandwiches
potato pesto salad
broccoli with roasted red peppers and tomatoes
French lentil soup
beluga lentil soup
chickpea soup
spicy green bean salad
3 bean soup
split pea soup
Jacob's cattle baked beans
elbow pasta salad with peas and carrots
wild rice salad with apricots and ginger
Mulligatawny soup
garlic and leek soup
vegetable soup
carrot dill sushi
cucumber sushi
spicy tuna sushi
mixed veggie sushi
roasted chicken
chicken satay

The word started getting around, and business started picking up. Larry's optimism-meter rose from guarded to cautious at the very least. Receipts were increasing to the point where he could see them operating through mid-October with no additional seed money, and donations kept coming in slowly but steadily each day. They *would* have enough to make a sizable contribution to the Westside Pantry, if they wanted to go that route, and still keep some money aside for their own program, as Larry had hoped. The more they brought in, the more they could do themselves in the winter.

Larry knew that Bill's "cooking up a storm" stint for the café would be an interim thing; he realized that soon Bill would have to take time to wrestle with the employment issue one way or the other. Some part of Bill, Larry also knew, wished that he could just cook his way into prosperity for the café, the soup kitchen, and himself, but at this point in the season that was simply not going to happen. Bill turned to job seeking, putting his resume together and so on, things he needed to focus on before making the big push in the kitchen for the Soup with Sinatra event.

Meanwhile, Larry, Alex, and Monica designed some T-shirts for the Common Good, something Larry realized they should have done a long time ago, when lots of tourists were stopping by to use the Wi-Fi and get their free coffee. For once he had actually been too conservative. They had the logo in the front with a powder blue color for the inside of the pot just like on the Web site, along with the words Southwest Harbor, Maine. On the back they had a script version of "Fearless Optimism in a Bowl," thinking that might be a real conversation starter when people read it as the wearer walked by. The management team all got free shirts, and looked great in them.

Larry had one more project in which to enlist his nephew Ben. It was a standard feature of island businesses to have signs directing tourists to their locations; these were standardized roadside signs approved by the Maine Department of Transportation that simply had the name of the business and its distance from that point. They had discussed having such a sign for the Common Good Café, to guide people from the main road, 102, down to Seawall, but it was expensive to get signs made, and it took a long time to go through channels and arrange for such a sign, time they did not have. He decided a wildcat sign was in order for the café, modeled on the state signs. He found the perfect location, scoped out the terrain, and picked midnight on the Sunday before Labor Day for the installation ceremony (there would be a full moon that night). When they got to the site and were ready to pound in the fence post with the small sledgehammer they had brought, they saw a car coming toward them. "Should we jump in the ditch and hide?" asked Ben frantically. Larry looked at the ditch, pretty deep and mucky. He looked at the car, and saw no sign that it was the police, and shook his head no. The car rolled by harmlessly, the installation went smoothly, and off they sped.

"Hey," said Larry to Ben, laughing at himself; "Good job, man. Soon hoards of tourists could be taking that left turn and heading down to the café!" This all reminded Larry of what he and his friends in the late sixties used to call a micro-revolutionary act. (Much later Larry found out ironically that the land they put the sign on belonged not to the state right of way as he had thought, but to his good friend Ned Butler! They could have done all this in broad daylight.)

Speaking of micro-revolutionary acts, Larry kept his appointment at Tom's Terrific Tattoo parlor. The whole process took an hour and Larry was pleased as punch with the results. It would have been much faster if he had settled for just black lines, but he wanted the blue color in the pot, too. He had waited seventy-one years to get a tattoo and found that he liked having it. He was tickled by having to sign a paper saying he was getting the tattoo of his own free will, was not impaired by drugs or alcohol, absolved Tom's Terrific Tattoo of all liability, and so on. He was even more tickled to find that Tom's assistant, following company policy no doubt, had placed in the middle of Larry's back car hatch a complimentary condom with Tom's Terrific Tattoo Parlor printed on the wrapper. "Wow," thought Larry after he had figured out where it came from, "that will come in handy ... *not!*"

When folks saw the tattoo on his left forearm the universal first response was, "Is that real?" Larry would calmly say it was real and invite the more adventurous to touch it. He had not thought that the tattoo would provide this much amusement for him. Bill was duly impressed, and saw it as sign of re-newed resolve and commitment

Larry's tattoo. Is it real?

by Larry, which Larry understood and had even somewhat anticipated. Actually for Larry personally, the tattoo represented a kind of insurance policy, a guarantee that he would always be reminded of the Common Good Soup Kitchen and this time in his life, even if the project folded. Mostly he just liked the way it looked on his arm.

Larry remembered with exquisite clarity driving down to Seawall with Franny, shortly after noon on Friday, September 25. It was a sunlit Sep-tember afternoon, and he was trying not to be too anxious, driving at the speed limit or below, an agonizingly slow two-mile trip. "Will the people come?" he wondered, palms starting to sweat just a bit as they passed the camp supply store and swung around the curve to Seawall proper. Cars were in fact all over the place in the parking lot and his belly suddenly felt very warm.

Don was a great performer, the soup and salads Bill had whipped up were of course great, and the staff was great. There were several large groups from senior residences and day programs and many familiar faces among the hundred or so folks in attendance. Professional clown and balloon artist Kathy Gurak, aka Noodles, filled the room with ador-able balloon hats and flowers and animals. Their faithful journalist sup-porter, Nan Lincoln of the *Bar Harbor Times*, was there with her mom and her camera, covering the event live. Franny had an especially great time, grooving on the music and the ocean view, sunlight dancing on the waves, the friends at their table, and she and Larry did a small dance together to the smiles of the crowd. The volunteers were out in good number and were ecstatic at the crowd and the good vibes. The event was free, but there was a donation bowl for those who wanted to contribute and it was pretty packed with greenbacks. The first community soup event was on the books now. Bill stayed chained to the stove, the chef in his cave by the fire, almost the entire time, but came out in his overalls smiling near the end, looked at the crowd of happy faces, and said to Larry, "I think we finally got to the goal line."

"I was thinking more home run," said Larry, sticking with the baseball metaphor. "Whatever," laughed Bill, "we scored big, we walked the walk."

Larry could not disagree with that.

Sometime later that day Larry again had the experience of being enlightened by seeing the obvious. Soup with Sinatra would not be just a special event, as they had initially thought of it, but would be the model for their standard operation in the winter. They would build a program around soup events, drawing the community in with healthful, yummy free soups and salads and live music or other entertainment. People could take soup home after the events, and the Common Good delivery crew could assemble on that day to pick up the soup and make the deliveries. The community events, the sit down soup kitchen, and the soup delivery would happen on a regular basis and all basically out of one afternoon. Because they had started with deliveries, a very important and unique function, he had not seen how regular "come on down" soup kitchen events were the key to making the program viable and visible in the community and how well these events dovetailed with the delivery program. He had been wearing blinders and it had taken Hannah's suggestion and then the actual event to totally remove them to where he could truly see what was right in front of him. They would do as many of these soup events as they could manage in the winter; *that* would be the winter plan, what the contribution kitty was for. It seemed very do-able to Larry at this point to pull off a soup event as often as once a month, November through April. His optimism moved up another notch—it was clearly in the fearless range now.

15

October:
Cornucopia for the Common Good

One morning while driving out to the blueberry field as the sun rose, Larry got the idea for one more fall fund-raiser, an entertainment-focused one. He knew that he could draw on Alex's talents here: she was not only a talented musical performer, she also produced Broadway style shows every summer for the Summer Festival of the Arts—it was the finale highlight of the program every year. He approached Alex; she thought that she could put together a team, and thus "Broadway by the Sea" was born. They settled on a date, Saturday, October 10, kind of their last hurrah, but it would put some

Dr. Jeffrey Knowles. His talks on nutrition launched the Common Good educational events.

money in the kitty for the winter and also be a lot of fun. They also settled on Friday, October 16 as the last day of daily café operation.

Larry focused on getting the PR machine working full force for "Broadway by the Sea." The press release went out, so that it would appear in the papers on the Thursday before the event, a little tight but very fresh in people's minds as something to do on the upcoming weekend. Larry again turned to Ben, this time to do a cool graphic for the flyer. Since Ben was close in age to the entourage, he was spending a lot of time over at their place anyway, and he definitely felt a strong desire for the event to be a success, so this was giving him a labor of love that also involved computer graphics. Ben dove in and came up with computer-based graphics from the classic Broadway playbill design and put together a dynamite poster. They also took some great publicity shots of Alex. Once again the entourage and the volunteers plastered the island with flyers. Larry told them that he did not want to be able to go anywhere in town, or walk past any window, without seeing that poster. The godfather thing might indeed have been getting to him a bit.

Poster for "Broadway by the Sea"

An interesting opportunity now came up for Bill: College of the Atlantic was having a three-day weekend conference entitled *Food For Thought, Time for Action: Sustainable Food, Farming and Fisheries for the 21st Century*. Bill thought that he could learn a lot, that attending the conference would help him gain knowledge and contacts useful to the soup kitchen as well as himself. Larry agreed. Bill armed himself with copies of his resume and set off on Friday afternoon, October 2. Larry received a phone call from a somewhat agitated Bill that night after 9 p.m. Lots of people were asking Bill questions about the Common Good's organizational structure, nonprofit and profit income streams, programs, winter plans, overall mission, and so on. "I can't answer these questions that people are throwing at me. We need to meet next week and figure out what we're doing here."

Larry was calm. "Actually, I think we do have a pretty good idea of what we are doing, have a lot of this worked out, at least I think we do." He offered to prepare a briefing portfolio for Bill. Bill protested that he did not really need to do that, but Larry said that was no problem, he would drop off the briefing statement at Bill's house the next morning, so that Bill could read it over before the day began and be in a position to answer the questions. *This* was the time to give Bill his briefing folder, otherwise Bill would have a miserable weekend, at sea in Bar Harbor without a life raft or a kayak, or even a tiny little dinghy. Larry was in fact enlightened by Bill's predicament; Bill had either produced or col-laborated on just about every idea the Common Good program had, but Bill had not been the one to put them on paper, nor did he have them in the front of his mind all the time as Larry did. He produced them and then went to wrestle with day-to-day issues in the kitchen. Of course he needed a "refresher course," and this would improve com-munication between Bill and Larry as well.

Larry now perused his computer files of Common Good folders and documents, figuring out which ones to print out or cut and paste from to cover all the bases for Bill. He was a bit stunned at the volume of material he had produced, never having really reviewed it this way be-fore. In the Common Good Community folder there were no less than eighty-five documents: flyers, handouts, sign ups, information sheets, policy statements, press releases, you name it. There were an additional thirty-eight in the My Documents folder. He got really curious now, his scientific quantitative spirit aroused. He knew there were also many e-mails related to the project that never were documents: ninety that had gone out to the whole Common Good Contact list, an additional seventy-five that had gone to their Web site person Jennie, and thirty-five that had gone to James when they were discussing co-op and other start-up issues early on. He stopped counting at this point. This was the first time he had ever begun to think of himself as the Energizer bunny. Actually he realized it was his ability to react quickly, to be totally proactive that had enabled the Common Good to develop from scratch as quickly as it had, get to this point at least. He knew that it was his therapist, the "divine Ms. L," Laurie Laviolette, Licensed Clinical Social Worker, who had enabled him to become the Energizer bunny. She had not only helped him out of a serious depression he had fallen into several years earlier but had worked with him to identify the thought processes that had held him back to an extent most of his life, even when he was feeling good. She turned him from having problems with procrastination to being Mr. Proactive himself. Once again he silently thanked the divine Ms. L.

Larry proceeded immediately to put together a packet for Bill, mostly cutting and pasting, but wrote up a new summary of their profit-nonprofit structure and included a special section for Bill's eyes alone on problems and issues that he thought they really did need to discuss. These included soup production plans for the winter, beefing up and organizing the delivery program, finally walking the walk to start producing recipe guides and food prep demonstrations, and encouraging Bill to look at presenting cooking classes, catering, and packaged food sales as money making possibilities. He did end staying up quite late, but this was important, this was no boom box request fiasco.

He delivered the packet to Bill's kitchen on the way to walk the dog the next morning before 7 a.m. Bill called him from Bar Harbor, at 8:45 or so, very elated and a bit surprised. "I read the stuff over during breakfast," he said. "It's all here. Thank you. You answered all the questions. I don't think you left anything out. I think you have the makings of a real handout here, do you mind if I make copies, people may be asking for them, they really are curious about what we are doing." Larry said that for sure he did not mind, that he was glad that people were curious and wished Bill a nice day.

Something about doing all this stirred up more ferment in Larry's brain, especially when it came to the one part of the mission statement they had hardly touched, the biggest challenge of all. With the resources they were beginning to accumulate they could do the community part of the mission and the soup kitchen part of the mission and maybe even a good chunk of the education part. However, breaking through the cultural food barrier part, really becoming an antidote to Food, Inc. and helping to put organic, whole food, and local food production on a mainstream footing—that was a lot harder, maybe a pipe dream, and would require more resources. He brainstormed the idea of creating a line of healthy, natural, locally-based fast food. He detailed it in an email to his friend Jane Mannette, the ultimate entrepreneur, who happened to be in Nigeria at the time. He proposed that they could not only create such a food line but ultimately train others in the same approach, and start a healthy fast food chain that spread across the country, each franchise encouraging its own particular local food producers. They would become, in effect, the anti-McDonald's.

Two days later Larry received an e-mail announcement from the Echoing Green foundation, forwarded by his son Andy in New York. It seemed that the Echoing Green foundation existed for one fundamental purpose: to provide seed money to people with an innovative idea that could change the world and have a major impact on society. They wanted to support "social entrepreneurs." If you were established, if you had something already up and running for a while, if your goals were laudable but modest, then their fellowship program was not for you. If you were a couple of old dudes that came out of the woods with an idea to change the food habits of a nation, just starting from scratch with no resources, or a student ready to drop out of grad school to pursue your dream, then you might be just the person for whom the Echoing Green folks were looking. Larry was flabbergasted. Some place deep in his soul lit up, was set on fire. One of the things that really had stayed with Larry, both saddening him and stiffening his resolve, was something Bill had said the morning after he had been laid off by Chow Maine: "Here I am, just a fifty-six-year-old unemployed guy again; who was I to think I could change the world?" The Echoing Green people were looking to support little guys with big ideas. Talk about fearless optimism, talk about fueling hope and dreams. He filled out their preliminary online diagnostic questionnaire to see if they were appropriate candidates for an Echoing Green fellowship grant: they scored nineteen out of twenty! The only place they were lacking was they had not done any research to see if anyone else was pursuing the same idea. With no whole food, local food, fast food chain on any strip mall he had ever seen, Larry was pretty sure this was not really a problem. Of course they would apply. The Echoing Green program almost literally came out of the blue for Larry and its existence validated what Bill and he and been down deep fighting for, dreaming about. It vindicated all their efforts for Larry. He was often on the verge of joyous tears that morning, and the good feeling echoing deep down inside his belly lasted all day.

Bill returned from the conference full of ideas and with a different sense of the Common Good project; he now saw the Common Good community as part of a larger and growing movement to promote local foods and sustainable agriculture. He did not know how this would play out for him personally, but it was exciting to be part of it. Bill said that he would probably be doing some traveling, at least along the Maine coast, maybe further south, checking out opportunities. He also said that he did not want to be the "face" of the soup kitchen any longer, that it was bigger than him, that it was time for others to step up. He had taken his picture down and wanted his role played down in the press from now on, pointing out that Larry and the volunteers were the real face of the organization. Larry said that he understood that, but that even after he was no longer a general and no longer president and had retired to Mount Vernon, George Washington was still the father of our country and still is for that matter. Likewise, Bill was the father of the soup kitchen no matter what he did or did not do from here on.

Larry also said that he understood that Bill would now make soup or other food when he could, contribute as he could, but no longer be *the* go-to guy for their basic soup production, just cook when he was in town and available. Bill concurred. Who would they look to then, to be the head chef for soup production? Bill said that maybe the best way to run the program was with volunteer chefs, one way or the other. Larry said that Bill might be on to something there, and that he would mull it over very seriously.

Resources and positive input began to pour into the Common Good at a dizzying pace. A couple that had stopped at the café one day happened to be sign makers with their own business in New Hampshire; they offered to make new signs for the Common Good to replace the crude hand-lettered ones that were at the café and on the road. They hooked up with Alex via e-mail, a package arrived soon afterwards via UPS, and voila: the scruffy amateur signs had been replaced by two spiffy professional signs free of charge. A local restaurant contacted Larry to say that they did wine tastings where a percentage of the take went to charity, and that the soup kitchen would be their next recipient. Lobsters were bestowed on the café by a local lobsterman, as was a ton of produce from various local farmers: potatoes, squash, carrots, kale, cabbages, you name it. Larry got a voicemail message from someone who lived on Seawall Road who wanted to know how to make out a check to their 501(c)(3) fiscal sponsor; Larry was happy to call him back and a nice check for $250 soon went out to the Good Ideas program for the benefit of the Common Good. Almost every day a new person called or dropped in to the café and left their name, wanting to be added to the volunteer list; a fall and winter cadre was developing that would be more than ample person power to replace those who left after the summer season. Larry got an e-mail from the Blue Hill co-op enquiring as to whether Dr. Knowles might be willing to give a talk out there; their fledgling educational efforts were beginning to have a ripple effect as well.

Dr. Knowles in fact gave his second talk on October 8, again with a good crowd, a lively discussion, and good lunch business. The talk focused on the necessary minerals and vitamins that we need and how to get them. He emphasized that extracted or synthetic vitamins and minerals in pills and supplements were typically only a small part of the substances as they existed in food products themselves, that the vitamins and minerals were actually part of larger complexes including many important micro-nutrients that were left out of the extracted products. He argued that you should get your vitamins and minerals in the food substances themselves that contain them. He even made the heretical-sounding statement that as far as cooking oils were concerned there was nothing really better for you than a bit of butter! He further made the point that the nutritional quality of food, especially its micro-nutrient content, ultimately depended on the quality of the soil in which the food was grown or the food that the animals that you were consuming part of ate. It was one of the best overall rationales for "going organic" that Larry had ever heard, actually.

A new couple showed up at the café one day, Richard Grossinger and Lindy Hough. They had a house on Seawall Road too and they owned a publishing company in Berkeley, California, where they lived most of the year. They were very impressed with the Common Good Café, and had been fans of Bill's cooking from his Seaweed Café days. They had organized their company to benefit charities, along the lines of the Paul Newman model, and down the road they would certainly like to help the soup kitchen. Richard thought that the entire Seawall space could become a spiritual and eco-tourist center if the right people came along: the spot was unique, had spectacular ocean views, and was adjacent to the park, salt water, and marsh and fresh water. There were some beautiful hardwood forest sections too, and five distinct ecological zones within the twelve acres or so that comprised the property. The Seawall area had even been included in a book devoted to Roger Tory Peterson's ten best bird-watching areas in North America. Its potential as an eco-tourism site was unlimited and maybe he, Richard, could get some people interested in the idea. Larry concurred, and Dave was very energized when Larry passed this information on to him.

Larry got another call out of the blue as it were, from one Allison Bell. The Tremont Congregational Church, of which she was a member, was interested in working with the Common Good program. This was huge, because that church was particularly known on the island for doing good works and for holding the best community suppers around, had a very progressive, well-liked, and socially conscious reverend and a very nice facility for dining and cooking as well; to top it off they were just about five minutes down the road and around the bend from Seawall. There could be no better group for the Common Good to hook up with in terms of increasing their outreach to the local community both in terms of finding clients and recruiting volunteers. This connection could ultimately be like having their ten Jonis. Later, he would learn that the church was not only interested in working with the soup kitchen, it would be willing to consider having soup kitchen events at the church facility. The Common Good was going to have another option for the winter.

Then George Swanson, the folksinger and social activist who lived down the road from Larry, came into the café and announced that he was putting on a performance of *The Threepenny Opera* and the soup kitchen would get a percent of the profits, to be shared among a group of charities. The Common Good's cut alone would be worth over four hundred dollars—manna from heaven, as it were, coming in with no expenses and no effort on their part!

Meanwhile, the Broadway by the Sea night was coming upon them fast, and something had to be put in place for food production. Alternative lead chef possibilities did not pan out, and they were down to doing some kind of catering or asking Bill to strap on the apron one more time for a big event, interrupting his "stand down" program, as it were. Monica became the lynchpin in convincing Bill to step up for this event; he really respected her dedication to the program and the energy she was putting into it, and he could not refuse her impassioned appeal. The papers came out and did huge spreads in their arts sections on the event, and as the day of the event dawned the crew knew it was going to be big. But they were in a bind because the volunteer situation was still a bit in transition from summer to winter crew, and only a few people had responded to the e-mail call for help for this event. Larry got a call in the early afternoon from Alex saying they were going to be terribly shorthanded if they did not get more help down at Seawall later that day. Larry thought: "Holy Hi-Ho Silver, we need to get more volunteers for tonight? What can be done at this point?" Then he thought: "if you are the godfather in this town, Larry, you can get volunteers for tonight."

E-mails would be useless at this point, and a couple of phone calls led nowhere. Then Larry realized he knew where lots of volunteers were, actually. They were at Oktoberfest, on the grounds of the Smugglers Den Campground just outside of town. It was a sunny day and everyone would be there. It was time for the godfather to make some personal calls, literally put the arm on people. So Larry headed down there, paid his admission fee, made the rounds from the beer tent to the music tent to the food tent, and sure enough when Oktoberfest was over there were five more volunteers headed down to Seawall. It was a good thing too, because the crowd ultimately filled every nook and cranny of the place. Jill and her husband Bob, plucked from the Oktoberfest, energetically worked to help set up and then were behind the scenes in the kitchen working with smiles on their faces all night.

Alex had recruited a cast of three other singers and a musical director to play keyboard. They had rehearsed assiduously. They performed eight different numbers from shows that ranged from *Les Miserables* to *Little Shop of Horrors* to *Forever Plaid*. They got sustained applause and bravos. The place was indeed packed to the rafters. People also raved about the food, several saying that it topped anything they had eaten at any local restaurants. With Alex on stage Monica ended up working like a whirlwind; she was the glue that held the whole food service part of the event together, under great pressure. At the end she was able to come off working the floor and the kitchen for about ninety seconds so that she and Alex could sing a song they had written to Bill and Larry about the Common Good. They played ukuleles to accompany themselves, and it was a hoot.

There was over $1,300 in cash and checks in the bowl when they were done, and probably many more thousands in good will had been credited that night. Before he left, a substantial fellow with a solid quiet demeanor, dressed in overalls, approached Larry and asked if he could meet with him to discuss the Common Good Soup Kitchen Community program. Larry, purely out of generosity of spirit, agreed and they set up a meeting for early Monday morning down at the café: no harm in talking to an interested well-wisher. The next day, Sunday, as they all basked in the afterglow of success, Monica said to Larry: "This guy just showed up and washed dishes for over two hours and then disappeared and we did not even get his name. Do you know who he was? Do you know anything about this?" Larry had nary a clue, at least not then.

On Monday morning the solid fellow with the quiet demeanor showed up right on time down at Seawall, as did Larry. "Aha, you are the phantom dishwasher!" Larry blurted out.

"Guilty as charged," was the reply. "I love to wash dishes, I will be your dishwasher for all your events, you can count on it."

His name was Matt Gerald; he owned Sweetpea Farms outside of Bar Harbor, and he was for real. He had read the mission statement, checked out the Web site, and was very impressed with the Common Good Soup Kitchen's philosophy. Other food pantries didn't really know what to do with local produce and gave out the usual pre-packaged food that did not in any way promote a healthy diet; the Common Good was the program he had been looking for all these years. He admired what they were trying to do and wanted to work for them. He had greenhouse space and next year could grow vegetables for them all winter, would have planted for this winter if he had known about it in advance. He had free-range chickens he would donate when the time was right. He was well connected with the local, organic agricultural community, which would be very eager to work with the Common Good program. He asked Larry if they had a farmer on their board, and Larry said no, not up to this point—but maybe they do now, and Matt agreed to serve in that capacity. Larry drove down Seawall Road to his home, shaking his head in wonderment: "Now I know how women feel when they meet that special man. Mr. Right just walked into my life. All of our lives."

The dizzying pace continued. A couple of days later there was a volunteer meeting to discuss winter plans. With a winter war chest in the soup kitchen account in the neighborhood of six thousand dollars, new volunteers coming in for the winter, and Matt Gerald as a major new man on the ground, they had some real options now. Perhaps they could work out something with Dave and Vickie to still use Seawall in the winter, on an event by event basis, paying a fee for daily use. Perhaps they could move winter operations to the Tremont Congregational Church, hold soup events there. In any event Larry would propose starting their winter program during the first week in November and going through the end of April; these were the off-season months, tourist wise and job-wise, and they also coincided with the Westside Food Pantry's months of operation. The gist of the volunteer meeting discussion was that they should try and maintain a presence at Seawall since people really liked that space and they had lots of momentum going there. All were also in favor of pursuing the idea of establishing a cadre of volunteer chefs. Bill offered to do a "soup intensive," a training program in his cooking methods over a weekend, to help promote the volunteer chef program and also reach out to other programs in the area, in order to help expose their chefs to some new approaches to cooking in volume. Larry thought this was a capital idea and so did everyone else, and eventually they settled on the first weekend after Thanksgiving for the intensive to occur.

There was one more thing Larry had to check out right now. There was a program of some sort, presumably supported by the state, to establish community warming centers where people could go during the day in winter and be warm while dialing down and saving on fuel costs at their homes. Maybe the soup kitchen/café space could qualify and get some financial help this way? After chasing this lead for quite a while, he ended up speaking with Elena Scotti of the Campfire Coalition; as it turned out they did not fund warming centers, but she invited Larry to a meeting of local volunteer organizations that the Campfire Coalition was hosting the very next morning. Though this was a dead end for funding, Larry did attend the meeting and was quite glad that he had. For one thing he was impressed with how Elena had put the whole thing together. The Campfire Coalition ran the heating fuel assistance program without creating any new organization or administrative structure or core of volunteers. It piggybacked on existing service organizations and divided up the labor. The second thing was the personal impact on Larry of just sitting there among virtually all the service organizations of the island: the soup kitchen literally had a seat at the table now, and he was representing it. It made him feel that the Common Good Soup Kitchen was part of the community in a totally new way that felt remarkably good.

The winter plans now began to fall into place for real. Larry met with Dave the next day, and learned that he and Vickie had a fearless optimism of their own, that on that very day they were having heaters for winter installed at their own expense. They wanted to keep something going there in the winter, whatever it would take. Larry thanked them and said he would try to do some fund-raising to defray the heater installation costs, and they worked out a deal whereby the soup kitchen would simply pay the winter utility costs of their operation, and hopefully do some catering or other events that would be for profit and give Dave and Vickie a cut of those.

Larry then had one of his best thoughts in weeks, maybe since the whole thing started. They needed a coordinator for the volunteer chef program. Yes, people could come up with individual soups and salads that they made well, but somebody had to figure out who was doing what for each week, put it together and keep it together. He thought of Joni. She was committed to the Soup Kitchen, though so far she had only done deliveries. She worked three or four jobs in the summer, like so many other folks around there, but soon these would all end and she would have time in the off-season. She had a great interest in cooking and food. Larry now recalled that they had often exchanged recipes and that Joni was involved in volunteer fire department suppers for large groups of people. No one had deeper roots in the community than Joni, she never jaunted off to the Florida for the winter, and Larry knew her to be creative, enthusiastic, and conscientious to a fault. They had a long-standing, very easy relationship with one another, good communication. What better person could they find? Again the perfect solution to a problem was right under his nose, though in this case she had not been available until now that the season was winding down. When he broached this to Joni he knew for sure he had made the right choice. She figured that once November rolled around she would be able to do it, and they talked about how to structure things effectively. In less than a day she was brimming with ideas, good ideas. The winter program was real now, for sure. With a deal in place with Dave, some bucks in the bank, and Joni on board, they could and go for it: a soup event every week, November through April. He began to create the press releases and the flyers in his head.

Although the café was officially closed, as they geared up for the winter soup program to start in November, there was one more October event on the boards. Alex and Monica had two friends, Kat Chiffler and Liz Hylander, who were very committed to supporting the sustainable local agriculture movement. They had worked all summer on an organic farm in Southern Maine. They were coming up to spend a week or so with Alex, Monica, and Casey at the entourage house. They would be willing to give a talk about their experiences. Even better, they had a film. They had undertaken a bike tour several years ago that took them from Baltimore to Montreal over many months; they had stopped to work with and interview folks doing urban farming and working at urban area fresh market farm stands, and documented this on film. They would show their film, *Faces of the Farm*, there would be a discussion period, and they would serve some organic soup they had made. Another press release, with a picture provided by Alex, more flyers.

The day arrived and Larry received a call from Alex at around 11:15 a.m. "There are a lot of people here, more than we planned for, is there any way we can get more soup? We don't have near enough." Larry as at a loss at first, but again heard the voice in his head: "If you are really the godfather, you can get soup, even on this short notice." He reached out to Grumpy's, the breakfast and lunch place down at the marina near their house, operated by friends Steve White and Stacy Richards. They made soup, good soup. They listened to Larry's story and offered him a gallon of either split pea with ham or crab bisque. Larry selected the latter and less than fifteen minutes later he was walking into the café at Seawall with an additional gallon of soup. Alex was very happy but only mildly surprised; after all, Larry was the godfather of Southwest Harbor, and she expected no less. It is only much later that Larry thought, "Hey, you are not really the godfather of anything, it was a joke. How did you let the idea worm into your head that way?" He did have to admit that it was a joke that ended up being one heck of a motivator for him. Hmm, maybe the next self-help book sensation could be *Finding Your Inner Godfather.*

It happened that holding the movie event that week served another good purpose as well. It was a day when folks could come down and pick up some of the surplus food. They had lots of such surplus food on hand, the result of the October bounty. Matt had even donated a hundred-pound pumpkin from his field to grace the café's last days. There were lots of smaller, more transportable pie pumpkins too, as well as squash, potatoes, and kale. Larry had Monica make a list of what was available, put it out to the e-mail contacts, and asked them to spread the word to folks who could come by and pick up whatever they could use.

He got an e-mail from one Julia Ventresco, who ran a community supper program in Ellsworth called Everyone Eats. Hadley Friedman from the Simmering Pot in Blue Hill had passed on his e-mail about the surplus food to Julia. She came down on the movie day and Larry ran into her: she was straightening up with an armload of potatoes, facing him in the kitchen area as he entered. She smiled and said that she was Julia and he must be Larry. In that brief moment he experienced something unique and got a very powerful "instant message." Something in his brain just told him intuitively that he was looking at a very special, really good person, someone he would really want to know.

That same night he received an e-mail from Hadley of the Simmering Pot in Blue Hill, suggesting that the three of them meet to discuss establishing come sort of central food commissary for the community kitchen programs in Hancock County. They set up a meeting for the following Thursday morning, at the Maine Grind coffee shop in downtown Ellsworth. This worked out well for Larry because he could attend the meeting after his regular sunrise croquet match with his friend Perry at the nearby Woodlawn Museum court. Larry had just settled at a table with Hadley and Julia when Perry himself walked into the coffee shop and spied Larry. He smiled with surprise and came over to say hello, saying to Larry, "Oh, so this is the meeting you had to get to." His face said something else too, especially his eyes. His whole demeanor said nonverbally what Larry's nephew Anton had articulated. "So, Larry, you started a soup kitchen and now you are surrounded by beautiful women."

They got down to business, forming an instant mini-support group on the spot. They all had the same philosophy, the soup kitchen as a free community meal experience, not a handout to the poor. They all had to shop and chop and plan all week. They all were way overworked. The Simmering Pot and Everyone Eats rented space in church basements on an event-by-event basis, and thus had limited storage space and limited access. Hadley suggested somehow organizing a central commissary: it would give them storage space, it would allow economies of scale as they could buy in quantities for all three programs and any others that might develop or that might want to come under their umbrella. It would help local producers because they could sell in bigger quantities, maybe even devote greenhouse space to grow produce in winter. It would save a lot of time to have a central shopping team as well, maybe a coordinating chef person and purchasing agent who could put out suggestions based on what was plentiful and cheap that week.

A light went on for Larry. Matt had mentioned that he had contacts with someone high up in the US Department of Agriculture through a good friend. This would be the proposal to go the feds with for funding, ask them to fund a central commissary for all the programs in the county, each one of which would still operate locally in their community on a grassroots basis. Government funds would be a facilitating factor, but with local control still running the programs with local funds, a win-win situation. Whether this particular avenue panned out or not, co-operating to try to get funds for a central commissary was an idea worth pursuing and would help to forge an alliance between the three programs. They agreed to meet again and discuss this further, and temporarily adopted the name of Hancock County Community Kitchen Coordinating Committee, HCCKCC.

The next day Larry met with Alex and Monica down at Seawall; it was the eve of their departure. Larry, getting carried away with his American Revolution analogy, thought of Washington's farewell to his troops at Fraunces Tavern. They discussed the program, what worked and did not work, suggestions for improvements, and how they could get a running start for next year. Larry thanked them profoundly for their incredible contributions to the program that had kept it alive, and reviewed with them the upcoming plans. His final word was that he recognized that the most difficult part of the mission to fulfill was in fact breaking through the food culture barrier and getting the natural food movement really down to the mainstream, down to the level of the guys that were now getting their lunches (and often breakfasts and dinners as well) from the pizza rack at the gas station, reaching out successfully to the McDonald's constituency. If they had any thoughts on this, now or later, he would appreciate hearing them. *Their* final words were "Guess what? We have rented the house for next season already, we will be back in May, and we want to work for the Common Good next year too!"

"Wow," said Larry, "that's great, here I thought it was going to be *au revoir* but instead it is *à bientât*, see you again soon." They hugged.

On Halloween night the weather was unseasonably mild. Larry took Franny to Bar Harbor for a movie, but deliberately arrived a half hour early. He parked at the foot of Ledgelawn Avenue, which was blocked off to vehicular traffic and filled with trick-or-treaters, many in elaborate costumes. Residents of that street went all out for Halloween, lighting up their houses as if were Christmas, and creating a block party atmosphere. He enjoyed the scene and saying hello to people in costume as they strolled by, but his head was focused on the next day, the opening of the voucher season for the Westside Pantry. He had arranged with Barbara Campbell to set up a table to give out information about the soup kitchen to folks who showed up to get their food vouchers. The flyers were ready, the press releases were out. Larry had thought that they should approach people after they got their vouchers, when they would be more relaxed, task completed, no longer standing in line. He already had a folding table packed in the hatch of the car along with two folding chairs, just in case. They were ready to roll. Larry began to feel good, really, really good, deep down good. It was going to happen tomorrow. He had said so many times that they were going to hook up with the Westside Pantry this way, expand their client base, get the word out. Tomorrow it would actually happen.

Sunday morning he got to Harbor House early, just past 11:30. Some folks going in helped him carry the table and chairs up. He looked at the situation, and decided to set up in the hallway area. People who came out the door with their vouchers would have to go right by their table on the way to the stairs or the elevator. The lines in the waiting area began to fill up. They were walking the walk now. Volunteers Joni and Janice arrived and joined Larry to help tout the soup kitchen. Monica stopped by on her way out of town; he was glad that she could be there to see the voucher line that looked to be over a hundred strong, to see the program that that she had helped keep alive now on the threshold of fruition. Another goodbye hug and she took off for New Hampshire with her soon-to-be boyfriend, BJ.

As people came out of the voucher room, Larry, Joni, and Janice not only handed out the flyers but also talked with many of the folks. They saw quizzical looks turn to smiles when they explained that that the soup events were free for the whole community, essentially lunch parties run by volunteers to which they were invited along with everyone else. Many people expressed an interest in volunteering themselves to help out, some with chefs experience—one in particular, Allen, in fact turned out be a master chef. The volunteer program was not only going to give them a reliable food production force, it was itself going to be a community building enterprise; it was going to let their "clients" help themselves and others, maybe the most valuable thing that the Common Good had to offer: again a simple thing right under their noses that Larry had not seen until that moment. The volunteer chef program was going to become a huge melborp, he could see it now. They were on the right track for sure, thought Larry, they *would* re-define what people thought of when they heard the words "soup kitchen," at least when it was the Common Good Soup Kitchen.

16
Seaweed:
Gift of Life, Food from Light

Seaweed as food! To this day the idea still strikes me as otherworldly, alien. I can conjure up a distant culture that thrives on an all-water planet, living on floating islands made of seaweed tangled together. Their buoyant air sacs support exotic palm trees, swaying above coves of pink and purple sand with ultra-white shells. These floating paradises are home to golden-colored lizards that the people (the Galactic Pirates) keep as pets. The Galactic Pirates prize these floating islands not only as a sanctuary but as a source of the sea vegetables that enrich their blood, allowing them to travel across galaxies without food or sleep to conduct raids and return safely with their booty. These lightning strikes from long distances leave their victims powerless to defend themselves, making the Galactic Pirates rulers of the night sky, all because of seaweed. Greenbeard himself, king of all pirates, will only receive the choicest of seaweeds as tribute from his men. As he holds court at Nori Cove you can see him gripping a mop of red, green, and brown seaweeds in his huge fist, thwacking his men on the head with it as a blessing for their tribute …

Being a chef from New England, seaweed as food seemed foreign but nonetheless carried a certain fascination, like any curious cuisine with considerable panache, such as Japanese or Korean. This "chef's curiosity" eventually led me to see what was right in front of me all my life, right in the Gulf of Maine. But most Americans I know, including a large percentage of chefs, look at sea vegetables as strictly *alien*, and as something that definitely does not belong on their plate. The only exception I can think of is sushi. Americans have embraced sushi. Nori sheets, which hold the sticky rice together to make the *maki* (roll), have become very popular. These sheets of nori are like microthin salty crackers processed into attractive glossy sheets. They are very civilized—nothing like the wild tangles of the raw thing with its viscous feel and strong sea-mineral smell. You would not see most Americans, even the "sushi" Americans, wanting to slog down a sea vegetable stew with cod and clams, but to me this is glorious. I imagine myself at an ancient Abenaki feast enjoying the hell out of myself.

Most American consumers are almost squeamish about foods like seaweed. Even more adventurous diners who suck down raw oysters think of sea vegetables as being somewhat unpalatable. The most common reaction to my culinary seaweed suggestions is "It's too fishy for me." But "fishy" has nothing to do with it. A broth made with kombu and vegetables has a briny, vegetable-mineral taste that is deeply satisfying and soothing to the stomach. The way some Americans react to such suggestions, you would think I asked them to dig into fish heads left out in the sun (which, by the way, is how "fish sauce" is actually made—you know, like in pad thai—surprise!).

The truth is, we have lost a lot on our way to American abundance. In the ancient world seaweed was valued so highly that it was offered to the gods in religious rituals. Most primate coastal tribes ate seaweed regularly and considered it medicinal. Medieval North Sea tribes took dulse seriously and had laws regulating its use.

Native American Know-How

Native American coastal tribes (pre-conquest, that is) made extensive use of seaweeds. The Native tribes of our Northwest states and British Columbia were the most evolved and creative in the use of seaweeds here in the Americas. The Haida tribes dried it like chips. They also fried it, which sounds fantastic. I haven't had the opportunity to use this method yet, but it's on my list of new tries. I'm sure health-food advocates, who comprise the strongest market for seaweed today, would want to hang me by my toes for that desire. But Mother Nature has given us "frying" and "seaweed," so just like Newman's Own organic coffee, it could be McDonald's new next big thing. You never know. On a contemporary Web site about the Haida tribes, there is a call for a return to this original native food, claiming that seaweed offers the broadest range of minerals of any food and that it contains the same minerals found in healthy human blood.

The Gulf of Maine had its own native coastal population, the Micmac and Abenaki tribes of Wabanaki Nation, which were considered clam cultures. In the summer season they would travel to the coast to feast on shellfish and other seafood. Their favorite was the soft-shelled clams. The shell mounds of Mount Desert Island are certainly evidence of that. I feel a kinship to my Abenaki and Micmac brothers. I too had a "clam culture." My routine entailed sunning and swimming at Singing Beach in Manchester, Massachusetts, on summer weekends. On the return trip to Lynn it was mandatory to stop in Ipswich to dine at a fry shack that overlooked the clam flats. There I would feast on what I considered then to be the king of all summer treats—fried clams with vinegar, salt, and ketchup finished with a root beer float with just the right amount of grit from the inevitable inclusion of sand. Today I am more akin to my native brothers' tastes with my new favorite dish—soft-shelled clams poached in seaweed and miso broth.

The Abenaki used seaweed to enhance the flavor of the clams and aid in their roasting. The clam bake was a great culinary method using blistering hot rocks to poach the freshly pulled clams wrapped in seaweed. For a chef this is pure brilliance—I mean, there are all kinds of things right with this. The Micmacs also had it right when they tossed seaweed into their wooden kettles along with clams, wild onions, and herbs—and again, a blistering hot rock—to make an original clam stew.

The Arrival of the Cod People,
Which Ultimately Led to the Big Mac and Fries

When the French, English, and Basques first came to the Gulf of Maine they didn't come for gold—they came for cod. In Europe it turned to gold. The Christian leaders of Europe around the fourteenth century proclaimed cod to be the preferred choice during times of abstention from meat, and the gold rush was on. Once the English found the Basques' prized fishing grounds on the outer banks of the Gulf of Maine and Newfoundland, they went about constructing one of the biggest fishing fleets in history. They brought with them their missionaries, their concept of aristocracy, and what they saw as a God-given ticket to the beauty and abundance of the New World. What they also brought with them on their hunt for the "sacred cod" was the beef they could eat on the meat days.

But the bigger and clumsier thing they brought was a perception. European scientists and nutritionists of the nineteenth century declared that protein, especially animal protein, was the "miraculous nutrient." It grew bigger and healthier people. Somehow that also made them better Christians. And I am assuming that beef was as delicious then as it is today. So it was a slam-dunk. Beef was crowned king in Europe. And subsequently, during the same century beef marched across the American plains in the wake of frontiersmen eager for buffalo pelts. Today cows dominate the American diet as well as the plains. Believe me, I love beef. A roast tenderloin on the bone with wasabi béarnaise knocks it out of the park for me. But enough is enough. Beef and dairy don't have to be in everything.

All I am saying is let's stop and look at the food sources around us here, on our coast. What we can take from the success of Japanese and French cuisines is not recipes but the art of cultivating what is grown around you. Seaweed is a powerful indigenous food that has been overlooked by the New England food culture. It could prove to be an invigorating, delicious tonic—actually, I am sure of it.

I wonder what could have been for the native people of the Gulf of Maine if they were unhindered by the European explorers. I imagine that a culinary culture could have evolved capable of rivaling the seafood culture of Japan. The northern islands of Japan where seaweed consumption is highest are on the same latitude as the Pacific Northwest and the Gulf of Maine. Today the Japanese are the biggest buyers of the seafood we don't think much of in our restaurants, such as sea urchin, sea cucumber, and seaweed.

We do know that the arrival of Europeans eclipsed any further development of the native cultures, but these newcomers also eclipsed their own culinary development by dragging the Western diet with them, which ultimately became the American diet with all its folly. I am not suggesting that European cuisines, especially French cuisine, are some kind of culprit. I would suggest rather that some ideas were misplaced in the heat of conquest for God and country. What American doctors call the "French paradox" illustrates the point. Though the French have a diet rich in beef, eggs, flour, and of course butter, they are overall much healthier than Americans. Not just that, they actually thrive. Their cuisine grew up around them for centuries. Maybe trying to import it to this landscape and the American culture doesn't really work that well. The native tribes had of course developed their cuisine out of their own surrounding environment, and were once the healthiest beings this continent ever saw. Could this be a clue?

Chef's Tour of Duty

It was during my time as a grunt line cook and working chef in Boston that I realized the following: (1) Some foods aren't good for you, including some that I love; (2) There are other food choices in the world.

My first real full-on chef's gig in Boston was at a restaurant called The Hermitage in The Institute of Contemporary Art. I had a habit of drinking milk for refreshment (as you already know, my grandfather had an ice cream fountain). In a short time I had chronic congestion problems that could last all winter. I thought it was from going in and out of the walk-in freezer. The boatload of lactic acid running through my brain was also slowing me down. The situation peaked when two guys from *Food and Wine* magazine interviewed me. I was so congested that I could hardly hear or talk. When I spoke I sounded like a duck drowning. The interview didn't go that well.

A chef friend of mine thought he knew what was wrong. I had a dairy allergy. Great! That made me the equivalent of a diabetic working in a candy factory. Dairy was in absolutely everything in the restaurant.

My chef friend, Ken Fornataro, knew a lot about Japanese food, and was very passionate about it. He convinced me to get off dairy and turned me on to a new type of meal—sushi rolls with nori, and miso soup with wasabi. My congestion cleared up and I never got sick like that again. With this result my curiosity about vegan foods and macrobiotics grew. After that I got most of my meals from a macrobiotic cafeteria down the block from The Hermitage, a habit I had to keep secret at the request of my boss. At this vegan cafeteria you were served a portion of seaweed such as wakame, hijiki, and arame. It was pickled, sautéed, and sprinkled dry as a condiment. That is when I acquired a taste for this food that was giving me more calcium than dairy was touted to give, without the side effects.

The next place I encountered seaweed was at the Five Seasons restaurant in Boston, owned by the Pell family, three brothers from Long Island who were wild about macrobiotics and good fresh seafood. They took a cuisine that was typically austere and turned it into exceptional-tasting food. The place had that buzz that only comes from hitting things just right, even though no one knew why. There I worked as a line cook and learned about their mad genius, and about using seaweed in classic dishes like chowder and salads.

But the place I learned the power of homegrown Japanese cuisine was at Gurumayi's ashram in Fallsburg, New York. I worked in her personal kitchen with a Japanese chef named Mikido. He was a serious dude about cuisine. He worked in a full-on martial arts costume and wooden sandals. He cut and chopped like a samurai. Like most Japanese chefs, he was into fermented food. He had experiments in his fridge that I still have no clue about. He was always sticking them in my face to try. Because of him I learned about Japanese tastes, especially seaweeds that were essential to Japanese living and health. They had seaweed for breakfast, seaweed teas, seaweed-based desserts, and even seaweed candy.

I became an all-out seaweed advocate at my own restaurant, Seaweed Café. You would think that would be a given considering the name. But my daughter Gillian actually named the restaurant when she was five. I was struggling to come up with a name. Gillian and I were hanging out at the seawall throwing crackers for the gulls. She picked up on my frustration and suggested that we call it Seaweed Café, handed me a bunch of rock weed, and insisted that the seagulls be invited. That did it. That was the name.

But the real reason I got into putting seaweed into the dressings and soups was because it was a local resource and it made sense.

A Seaweed Surprise

The reason why seaweed is so popular in the American health-food market is that the nutritionists got to it before the chefs. It is all-around incredible for your body. Seaweed offers the broadest range of minerals, nutrients, and vitamins of any food. It matches all the elements of healthy human blood. The Japanese diet is 15 percent seaweed. They have a very low incidence of diseases of the thyroid, lungs, or prostate. Heart disease is a fraction of the US rate. Professionals in food and science are still uncovering all kinds of health benefits from a diet containing seaweed. I can only present a list of benefits that particularly appeal to me as a chef always struggling with personal weight issues and my dairy allergy.

Including seaweed in your diet:

Aids in digestion and intestinal health. The mucilaginous gels promote healthy mucous membranes.

Protects the lining of the gastrointestinal tract and the mucosal lining of lungs.

The iodine promotes healthy stomach acid levels.

Regulates blood sugar and cholesterol levels.

Protects and improves liver and kidney function.

Is a natural appetite suppressant. The active ingredient fucoidan
in seaweed provides fucose to the cell receptors, along with
a feeling of well-being.
Serves as a valuable non-dairy source of calcium.

There are many more positive qualities of seaweed, too many to
list here. This should not be a surprise to us since we are all essentially
offspring of the ocean. We know more about land, sky, and stars than
we know about our oceans. The origins of our life are deep, deep, deep
in the ocean where no sunlight reaches. Yet there is light. Self-generated
light produces deep-sea life.

Seaweeds of Maine: You Carry the Sea in Your Blood

It's time to introduce our own local heroes, the seaweeds of the Gulf of
Maine. There are many types of seaweed, but these are our seaweeds.

All seaweeds are edible but not all are considered for cuisine. More
than 160 species are consumed around the world—fresh, dried, smoked,
pickled, and pulverized for condiments. What criteria do you use to
choose? I say the simplest method is to choose local.

There are a lot of seaweeds in the Gulf of Maine. Those that are the
most commonly harvested and available year-round in dried form are
wild Atlantic dulse, wakame, kombu, and nori.

Wild Atlantic Dulse is a type of red seaweed. Rich in potassium,
iodine, and iron, it has been used for centuries by North European cultures. A blood-red plant, it turns a deep purple when dried. Soft and
chewy, it is like hippie chewing tobacco. You can really put dulse in
anything. It's fantastic straight in salad. I enhance lobster stock with it.

Wild Atlantic Wakame is a green seaweed. Rich in calcium, vitamin
A, and vitamin B, this deep green leaf is very elegant and delicate in
broth. It is the top choice for miso soup in sushi bars. I put it in split pea
soup and minestrone—it matches basil well.

Wild Atlantic Kombu is a brown seaweed. Rich in iodine, potassium, iron, carotene, and mannitol, this deep-water plant is sturdy and
great for stocks. It is excellent for baked beans because of the glutamic

acid content, which makes the beans soft and silky and free from cracks while also reducing the tendency for them to produce flatulence.

Wild Atlantic Kelp is also a brown seaweed very similar to kombu. I love it in black bean soup and in a seafood stew with white beans.

Wild Atlantic Nori, also known as Laver, is a red seaweed, a cousin to Japanese nori. Out of all the seaweeds it is highest in B1, B6, B12, C, and E vitamins. When dried it takes on a deep black/purple hue and has a sweet, nutty flavor. Besides its obvious partnering with rice, nori is perfect for a sauté of penne and vegetables; it is recommended in salads and a recent great surprise—pasta sauce. The Irish eat it with fish and chips because it helps digest fats.

I would like to issue a culinary challenge to all seafood chefs and cooks, including myself. In the future, let's make seaweeds as much a part of our cuisine as lobster is today. That is exactly where we will start. Seaweed for life, man!

Epilogue
Sarah Hinckley
November 6, 2009

In journalism, descending on a scene at the time of celebration is what our jobs are about. We hear of the process when success is met. It is through our inquiries the finer details come to light. What we all long for is to be part of the process, from soup to nuts, capturing the feelings of elation and disappointment along the way.

Since moving from Mount Desert Island five years ago, I would call Bill on occasion to see what was going on in his life. There was

Joni Roths and Matt Gerald share a laugh while running the first winter soup event.

never a shortage of entertaining takes on island life and vivid reflections of a middle-aged, single father whose roots in the city of Boston caused him to stand out a bit.

A phone call in the spring of 2009 took a different turn. When I left MDI, Bill was in the midst of bringing a downtown restaurant to fruition. He told me how he had been laid off from there at the start of the year and while he was figuring out what to do next, he'd been making soup. Not just making soup, but delivering it to people within the community. Given what I knew of Bill and his ability to create something great from very little, I knew there was more brewing, but I really didn't know what.

A few months later I took a much-coveted trip to MDI. It was summer and I was determined to hit as many hiking trails in Acadia National

Park as possible during my long weekend visit. In those few months, Bill's soup making had moved locations. One pot of soup had become an organization with a name, a mission statement, a new location—on the ocean!—and there were more people involved. One in particular Bill was nearly giddy about was Larry Stettner.

Before donning my hiking shoes, I headed to the Seawall to see Bill. While trying to field suggestions from visitors, volunteers, and donors at the new Seawall location, he was also attempting to fill me in on the new developments. He explained how this one act of charitable intent, begun in his kitchen, had nearly taken over his life. If it weren't for Larry's enthusiasm and belief in this, he continued, we wouldn't be here right now.

Undeniably, I found the enthusiasm to be contagious. Sitting at a table in the dining room next to Bill as he jotted notes, I began to imagine how I might fit into the equation. This was a good thing, I could feel it, and had been looking for a sign to lead me in a new direction since leaving my job. What hit me at my core in learning more about the overall mission of the Common Good Soup Kitchen was not just feeding the community but creating a place of worship and appreciation for good, whole foods. One that featured local fare and exposed Maine people to Maine bounty for a more sustainable future.

Bill and Larry's ideas about educating people on how to eat healthfully and support their local food producers clicked with a personal dream I had carried deep inside for many years. After reading the extensive mission statement, I began to imagine how all the pieces of the puzzle could be put together and, if done successfully, what a wonderful model it could be for so many communities across the country.

Over the next few months Bill and I kept in sporadic touch. I moved back to Maine from Vermont and in with my sister's family, still searching and continuing to play out the possibility of being a part of the Common Good Community.

Connecting with Larry was the way to do so, Bill continued to tell me. So I wrote a long letter, explaining my small farm roots in western Maine and my passion for natural, healthy living, and asked how my skills in writing, photography, and cooking could be of assistance in helping the soup kitchen move forward with its mission. He answered my e-mail immediately, thanked me for the interest and said he would get back to me when he had time to read my e-mail more thoroughly.

He did get back to me: "Come cover our opening soup event," Larry followed up nearly three months later. After closing the summer café, the soup kitchen was about to start up again and serve the public one afternoon a week through the winter. "Bring your camera and note-book," Larry added, "and we'll see what develops from there."

There is a moment that stands out so clearly for me that opening day on November 6. I was standing in a transformed Annabelle's Seawall Dining Room (where I had my first job on Mount Desert Island nearly twenty years earlier) watching Bill and Larry greet one another in the midst of the celebration. It felt like someone had thrown a party and guests from all wings of life had been invited. Chuck and Emma were serenading the crowd with lively string music. There was conversation, silverware clinking on ceramic, and smiles on every face in the house.

Prior to Bill's arrival Larry made his way around the room, greet-ing visitors, a smile plastered on his face. It was his birthday, which few visitors were aware of, and he was indulging in a great gift. Eventually Larry, with eyes twinkling, planted himself at a table next to his wife, Franny. There was a bowl of soup in front of him into which he dipped occasionally as he drank up the atmosphere. When Larry noticed Bill, who had snuck in through the back kitchen door to assess the scene, he got up from his seat. Among the crowd of at least eighty people, the two men joked about the parking problem Bill had encountered when he arrived. Their inside joke since securing the Seawall location had been that if parking ever got tight, they had succeeded. They were quiet for a moment and Larry extended his hand to Bill, "Look what you started, man," he said, eyes still twinkling. Bill tried not to absorb the credit, but in that moment there was a shared acknowledgement that dreams can come true, if you just believe. (Working your butt off to make it happen helps too, I guess.)

Epilogue

Not many people saw it, or heard what the two men were talking about, because they were too busy enjoying the soup, music, and company. For me, it brought a tear to my eye and a warm feeling to my heart. Movements begin with one or two people who believe in something better for their community, their world. They grow with volunteers who often have nothing more to give than their time and talents. Looking around at those filling the pots and stocking bowls, washing the dishes, tasting the soup, talking with neighbors not seen for a spell, and drinking up the view, I saw pieces of the puzzle beginning to fit perfectly into place.

APPENDIX A
The Common Good
Original Mission Statement

The Common Good Soup Kitchen Community and Co-op Mission

(May, 2009)

Continue to distribute free soups and whole food salads to senior residences and others in need, expanding to service more people as resources grow.

Provide local space to store and distribute raw whole grains and natural foods to local businesses and individuals.

Promote the use of local foods harvested from the sea as well as local produce.

Educate to teach easy preparation of whole foods and to promote dietary habits which foster health and wellness.

Help to provide jobs all year round.

Build and maintain a sense of community all year round through sponsoring community events and establishing an inviting space where local residents can always "meet, eat and greet."

Provide an avenue for seasonal residents to be involved in supporting the community they love by helping it thrive all year round.

Provide a model of green, eco-friendly living.

Provide affordable natural food through keeping our costs down and via discounts to Common Good club members.

Help other local charities and service organizations.

Produce healthy, delicious soup and whole food salads for sale to support our programs.

Operate a self-serve café whose revenues will support our programs, and that utilizes the skills of our master chef in preparing delicious natural food.

History of the Common Good Soup Kitchen Community Program

A modern day fable that happens to be true.

Once there was a young man named Bill Morrison. When our story begins young Bill was working as a chef in a bastion of high cuisine in Boston, USA. On his off days he was for some reason drawn to local places, on the fringe, that featured and promoted a macrobiotic, holistic, organic approach to food and its preparation. One day the people there said to young Bill: "What are you doing here? You are different, you are not one of us." The people at the bastion of high cuisine said to young Bill: "What are you doing wasting your time hanging around with those kooky macrobiotic people? Stick with us and follow your true vocation, learn your craft." Young Bill listened quietly, but he still thought that those macrobiotic people had something, and that from a culinary point of view that was where he belonged.

Time passed, things happened. Bill ended up cooking in an ashram, where they had the mindset and the resources for Bill to apply his culinary skills to cooking in a macrobiotic, holistically organized way. He was happy. More time passed: Bill worked as a private chef in Colorado; Bill and Mary McClaud had a daughter, Gillian; the family all moved to a small town on the coast of Maine. Over time, Bill opened three restaurants there, for others or himself. They were "mainstream" restaurants but he tried to incorporate macrobiotic and organic principles to the extent that he could. It was not always easy to get the food ingredients he desired, and he wished there were better sources. At some point he began to think that he might create a local storehouse of some kind to become one of those better sources.

Still more time passed, now it was the winter of 2009 and daughter Gillian had grown into a beautiful, talented young lady in high school, and not so young Bill found himself unemployed in the midst of a very hard time economy in that small town in Maine and in the good old USA. He thought that this might be the time to pursue what he had seen in his mind and dreamed of: the creation of a local co-op for the sale and distribution and preparation of natural, healthy foods. Politics would be kept out of it. Organic, macrobiotic ways of looking at food and concern for the role of diet in health and wellness had moved out of the fringe and were rapidly becoming mainstream, albeit in danger of being distorted by the supermarket mentality and the packaging industry.

Bill (aka the Lone Ranger) sought out his friend Larry (aka Tonto) as a sounding board, and Larry listened and said that what he heard was good. To make it happen would be a good thing, and might even be a possible thing.

Not long afterwards, Mary McClaud said to not so young Bill that in these hard times it would be nice to do something with his cooking skills for the community, maybe a community supper. Bill thought this was a good idea, but why not do something nice on a more regular basis, not just a one shot event. So the free Soup Kitchen was born in February 2009. Bill took a small amount of money donated each week and turned it into a large amount of whole grain based vegetarian, yummy soup. He read Paul Newman's book, *In Pursuit of the Common Good* and got even further inspired. He told Larry about the book and Larry read it too and was also inspired.

One day, Bill again was walking and talking with Larry and he said that the soup kitchen was good, but he would really like to begin working on the natural food co-op project. Larry replied: "I have been thinking about the implications of the soup thing. It seems to me you already have started working on the co-op." Bill thought a moment, and said: "By god, you're right, Kemo Sabe."

Original Handwritten Mission Statement:
Bill Morrison, February 16, 2009

The Soup Kitchen is a community service: "Food for the Soul, Fearless Optimism in a Bowl."

1. We will use natural whole foods, as many as possible being organic.

2. The type of soups we make will be mostly whole grains, beans, and vegetables, with no animal products and low sodium.
3. We will be happy to receive raw food contributions for the soup as well as funds.
4. The idea is to provide healthy soup to anybody that needs or wants it at no cost to them.

The model we would like to use is that of the soup kitchen of the 1930s. That is: No Politics, No Bull, Just Soup.

The Mission as of May 2009

1. To create an **all year round storehouse** of whole foods, local products and locally harvested food from the sea that services the community by making the basics of a healthier nutritional lifestyle locally available and more affordable. The foods stored and sold through the Common Good Co-op will include:

- raw foods such as beans, rice and grains in bulk without wasteful packaging;
- prepared foods such as soups, whole-grain salads, seaweed wrapped sushi rolls, oils, vinegars, etc, prepared without additives;
- organic foods, especially those produced in Maine; local and Maine produce and products (i.e. vegetables, eggs, fruits, beans and berries);
- seafood from local waters and the Gulf of Maine, from catches both small and large, as well as locally harvested seaweeds.

2. To serve as an **educational resource** in the use of whole foods to improve health and wellness and for more connection with our own local food producers and harvesters. Our educational programs will include:

- teaching about the vital role of whole and natural foods in a lifestyle that promotes health, wellness, and longevity;

- activities and programs that will help people "walk the walk" of a healthier lifestyle, not just talk the talk. These will include daily food prep demonstrations, mentoring, group meetings and hands on events, contests and recognition awards, rather than simply presenting lectures and written information;
- promoting knowledge and awareness of local farm and food sources;
- teaching techniques to new chefs and for easy and tasty food preparation at home utilizing available whole grains, rice and beans;
- on-the-spot education from chefs present at the co-op at the point of sale will guide customers in how to prepare what they buy;
- explaining the benefits of seaweed as a food source, how to utilize it in our diets and how our fishing community can harvest it locally.

3. To create a **focus for community** on an all year round basis. A small community such as ours in a seasonal economy tends to be fragmented by excessive workloads for the local population in the summer, and isolation in the trying times of winter. The Common Good Co-op and Soup Kitchen will help promote a sense of community by providing a convenient place for people to shop, snack, meet and greet; by providing programs that they can share in and by providing many volunteer opportunities for people to be involved in simply helping their neighbors prosper and enjoy a happier and healthier lifestyle, i.e. promote the common good:

- sit down cafe space open all year where people can sit together and have a cup of coffee/tea, try a bowl of soup, some salad or sushi;
- well-managed community bulletin board for promotion of local events and activities;
- cooking demonstrations that will draw people together;

- educational events that will do likewise;
- periodic public meetings and get togethers so that members of the community can present their ideas for discussion of how the co-op might further serve them and promote the common good;
- fun activities that bring people together in the off-season: midnight soup parties instead of early morning pajama madness, contests to guess how many raw beans are in the soup ingredient jar, or to see who knows the most Paul Newman trivia, or to predict how many pounds Bill or Larry will lose (or gain) by the end of the month on their current diets; Family Feud night based on surveys of co-op customers, Texas Hold-em tournaments with different varieties of beans as chips, pot-lucks with live music for people to show off recipes made with food purchased from the co-op, etc.

4. Create a model for a **greener approach for the future** in our community. We are reaching a tipping point in our larger society where people are increasingly drawn to the realization that we cannot continue to use up the resources of our environment at the current rate. The show is over, we can't afford it any longer. A small community such as ours can show the way for the larger society by being more eco-friendly in myriad ways. The entire Common Good operation will be organized and run in a way that is transparently minimum waste, maximum utilization:

- using inverted model of market for more efficient space utilization and discouragement of wasteful packaging. The usual retail space is set up with a closed storage/warehouse area behind or separate from the service retail space. As products compete for retail space, the packaging gets bigger and bolder, outweighing the cost of the food itself! In the inverted model the storage space and the food preparation and kitchen space are integrated into and are part of the retail space. Bulk food system allows storage space and customer self service space to be essentially one. There is one fluid space mimicking a common street market style;

- labeling on shelves and containers to make consumers precisely aware of the source of their foods;
- bulk storage greatly reduces plastic and glass consumption and the need for subsequent recycling;
- some form of recycling program for customer convenience will be incorporated into the operation;
- incentives for box and bag recycling/reusable bags;
- using the same foods for sale as raw and in food preparation by chefs greatly reduces the problem of outdated produce so rampant in conventional supermarkets;
- distributing our vegetable trimmings and organic refuse as compost and as food sources for local farms and animal friends.

5. Help to promote a more **sustainable fishing community** by in essence forming a seafood co-op within the co-op:

- allow local restaurants and individual residents to buy directly from the local producers, rather than having to look to Portland, Boston or wherever;
- provide a place for local fisherman to sell their catch, no matter how intermittent or small;
- promote the local harvesting of new foods from the sea, such as seaweed and other sea vegetables.

6. Provide **economic benefits** to local residents:

- keeping overhead costs down and buying wisely in bulk makes "natural" foods much more affordable to consumers to begin with;
- distributing some portion of income back to co-op member consumers in the form of rebates further lowers their food costs;

- providing free recipes and cooking demonstrations shows people how to prepare healthy and satisfying meals at low cost from ingredients locally available;
- donating goods, services and/or a portion of surplus income to help local charities and nonprofit service organizations;
- providing year round jobs with decent pay right here: in a small community even a half dozen new jobs can have a significant positive impact;
- train young chefs so that they can develop employable skills.

7. Continue to operate **The Soup Kitchen:**

- distribute free soup *and* salads in containers to senior residences and others on a weekly basis as is being done currently, expanding the program as resources permit; seniors deserve the most nutritionally sound, wholesome and appetizing food that we can provide, not just "food that we can give them on the cheap";
- serve up free soup/salads at the co-op itself at certain times and at other locations on appropriate occasions;
- make soup and salads available for sale in a variety of ways to encourage healthier eating styles and to provide income for the free soup distribution and other co-op activities.

Synergy: Although the above goals are listed separately, the activities of the co-op will typically meet several goals at the same time and will act to augment one another. When a co-op customer comes in to the cafe area and watches our chef prepare soup or salad from the available grains, and then sits down and eats with other customers and finds the food delicious and satisfying, that person is already sharing an experience with someone else in the community. They are starting to consume healthier, more nutritiously satisfying food. They are learning by observation how to prepare tasty and satisfying food from whole grains. They are deriving the economic benefit of an inexpensive meal. They are exposed by example to a more economical and ecologically sound approach to meal preparation: using satisfying food that is readily available and affordable rather than having a pre-set idea of what food one "needs" at a given time of the year, even if it has to come from Chile.

The Action Plan

1. File papers with state of Maine to quickly form a **nonprofit** corporation.
Begin the process of becoming a federally tax-exempt charitable and educational organization.

2. Raise **money and resources**
- Hold series of fund-raisers in which natural, yummy soups and salads are featured and information about program is presented.
- Ask for donations of cash, raw food, services, equipment, etc. by word of mouth and through newspaper article and other means. Bank account at BHBT already exists in the name of The Soup Kitchen to accept cash contributions.
- Invite contributions from founding, sustaining, and supporting members by personal contacts, small dinner party meetings, and fund-raising mail campaign. Ultimate goal is to recruit 100 sustaining members at a level of contribution of 1,000 or more each, thus providing a solid financial foundation for the Common Good to continue to serve the community.
- Identify federal, state, and private foundation funding sources as appropriate and apply for same.

3. Seek **consulting** help.
- Blue Hill Co-op has been in existence for over thirty years and has evolved to do many, though not all, of the things that are proposed here. They are eager to help us get started, and initial meetings with their general manager and the chef who initiated the Simmering Pot soup program in Blue Hill have already taken place.

- Several Web sites and publications that give invaluable information for co-op start-ups and operations have been identified.
- Local fishermen will be consulted as to their needs and interests.
- Maine Organic Farmer Association (MOFA) representatives will be consulted as to the role they might play as suppliers.
- *Operating a Nonprofit: A Guide for Dummies* is on hand.

4. Identify possible **locations:** Several locations for a storefront co-op currently for rent are being looked at on the Southwest Harbor side of the island. We expect to choose a location soon and be up and running in the summer of 2009.

5. Identify needed **personnel** to get up and running:
- Have start up board of directors in place to launch the co-op.
- Need one chef/buyer/general manager/visionary leader.
- Need one financial officer/accountant/bookkeeper/store manager.
- Need some hourly wage store personnel for sales, loading, etc.
- Need volunteers for food prep, stocking, bagging, fund-raising, education, promotion and PR, delivery of soup, events, etc.

6. Start-up strategy
- Open storefront when sufficient funds are on hand to commit to lease on co-op space and procure necessary equipment.
- Open Web site where people can learn about the Common Good and get information. (A Common Good volunteer who is a Web site designer has offered to build, maintain, and fund the Web site.)
- Start small and grow organically: i.e. start by selling and serving soups and salads currently being produced, both at the co-op and at other distribution points, providing the recipes for making these items, keeping inventory small at

first by simply selling the raw ingredients for the foods being produced, holding demonstrations for how to prepare these items.

- Expand products and services as resources permit and demands dictate.
- Include catering service as source of co-op income that utilizes the unique skills and reputation of our founding chef.
- Hold series of educational meetings from the get-go that will educate people as to health benefits of a different eating style, increase awareness of the co-op and its goals and hopefully bring in more resources and continued contributions.
- Hold large open public meeting to explain what the Common Good Co-op is about, get input, attract volunteers and attract funds.
- Organize multi-outlet fund raising campaign through mail, Internet, newspaper, small meetings and large meetings to obtain necessary start-up funds.

Appendix B
Locally Based, Healthy Fast Food:
Application to the Echoing Green Foundation

Larry Stettner and Bill Morrison: December 2009, phase 1.
Common Good Soup Kitchen Community, Southwest Harbor, Maine.
90K max award over two years.

What is your new, innovative idea to create lasting social change? Be clear, specific and jargon free in your answer.

We will produce nutrition-rich, delicious and affordable "fast food" from organic and local sources. We will open a Common Good Kitchen fast food restaurant, the "Anti-McDonald's." The superiority of our product will lead to a proliferation of Common Good Kitchens in Maine, thereby fostering growth of the already existing sophisticated but small local/organic Maine farming community. We will not only sell prepared food, but provide information for customers to make similar food at home. Our efforts will be well publicized. We will train chefs in our philosophy, techniques, and approach so that they can go back to their communities and do what we do. (We create out of what is available and affordable, rather than have pre-set recipes that might demand an ingredient from 6,000 miles away.) Thus, our model will replicate itself across the land, one franchise at a time, state, by state, by state. McDonald's and its ilk has fostered food production in this country that is over- centralized, and subject to contamination, and shaped diets that are nutritionally poor. Our program as it replicates will re-shape food production to be local and organically based and foster diets that promote wellness.

What drew you to this issue? When and how did you come up with your idea?

Chef Bill Morrison had long bemoaned the lack of local sources for organic produce, grains, and seafood in our town. He dreamed about opening a natural food storehouse and co-op in Southwest Harbor. In February 2009 he became unemployed; this might be the time to pursue that dream. He discussed how to bring this about with his friend Larry. Both men were acutely aware of the "politics" of food in the United States: the socio-cultural and economic divide between those who have the beliefs, the motivation, and the resources to seek out local and organic food sources and those who do not. They were determined that at least for their town, they would make every effort to bridge that gap, to make "natural" and local food affordable, accessible and attractive to all, one way or the other. They held a series of informal dinner meetings. Bill prepared some food from what was available and inexpensive. Abruptly one of the guests blurted out: "What *is* this? This is delicious!" Everyone concurred—such simple ingredients, so healthful so delicious! Bill and Larry looked at each other: this was the way to bridge the gap; delicious, healthful, prepared, affordable, fast food. They had their mission.

As specifically as possible, characterize the need for your organization. Use statistics and references.

Spoiled, by Nichols Fox, an expose of the meat industry; the recent film *Food, Inc*; the truly frightening article on genetically modified food in the recent issue of *The Urban Gardener*; the fact that 80 percent of the food on supermarket shelves is produced by five food companies across the whole country; rising rates of obesity and diabetes to almost epidemic proportions in the United States—this all points to something terribly wrong with our current food production and consumption system. When is the next outbreak of salmonella or e-coli or whatever from a centralized food source that contaminates food over a wide swath of states going to happen? Everyone who has bought one of the red rocks (a.k.a. tomatoes) at the supermarket and found them totally devoid of taste, let alone micronutrients, knows there is a problem. But alternative food sources are relatively scarce and prohibitively expensive for a majority of the population. The consciousness of the problem is there but the bold move to start tipping the balance away from the dangerously centralized and mechanized food production and the poor diets that derive from it has yet to occur.

What is the root cause of this problem? How does your idea tackle this root cause?

The root cause of this problem lies in the economic and social conditions that characterize post-industrial society in the United States. Large concentrated population centers and more efficient modern transportation, distribution, and agricultural production methods foster highly centralized, concentrated food production and distribution, whether it be cattle, poultry, corn, or tomatoes. This in turn fosters shoddy practices: whoever can produce and distribute more cheaply and effectively from the smallest number of central sources will dominate and make the most money. So what if the chickens or cows can't move or have to be laced with antibiotics? So what if the tomatoes are dry and tasteless? On the consumer end, work demands and living patterns are such that whoever can sell people food in the fastest and most convenient way will dominate. Our idea tackles this root cause by having a centralized philosophy and methods that promote a *de*-centralized food supply! Our Common Good chefs and food entrepreneurs will be trained and empowered to create healthy, affordable fast food from their own local sources, thus shifting the balance towards local, decentralized, quality production!

Help Echoing Green visualize what your organization will do. Describe the specific programs that your organization will engage in to deliver your long term outcomes.

We currently occupy the site of a former restaurant, with spacious commercial kitchen; there chef Bill will devote full time, sixty hours a week for him, to developing a food product line of natural, nutrition-rich soups and salads, contacting and encouraging local food producers and training Common Good chefs in our philosophy and techniques. We will serve these soups and salads at free "soup events" every week, deliver food to senior residences and others in need in our local community, and package food in containers with our distinctive logo to generate revenue through sales via distribution to retail food outlets throughout the region. All this activity and the exposure to truly delicious, nutritious, and affordable food will create enough interest to attract investors to open the first Common Good Kitchen fast food restaurant in Ellsworth, Maine, on the strip right next to all the other fast food chains, in the spring of 2012. The menu line, production techniques, suppliers, chefs and marketing to stimulate demand will have been created over the prior two years while we are in the process of holding community events and serving soup for free to many in need. Staggering Synergy!

Describe your long term desired outcomes. How will you measure your progress toward these outcomes?

What we desire is that the landscape be dotted with Common Good Kitchen fast food outlets from coast to coast and local farm production of every kind is booming in and around cities and towns all across the land. Spin offs from our success abound of course, and our style of food and food production has become mainstream; thus the health of the population improves as well as the quality of life. Idealistic young people drawn to organic and local farming can actually make a living. Locally the revenue from our fast food outlets, our packaged food, and the restaurant/natural food grocery we will then be operating will support the expansion of our training program for the Common Good Kitchen chefs and food entrepreneurs at our Southwest Harbor headquarters, which will be going full blast. Our targeted and measurable interim goal is to create at least one hundred different food products and train at least two dozen Common Good chef/entrepreneurs in the first two years to provide the base for the Common Good Kitchen healthy fast food movement. When we have attracted enough investment money to launch the first CGK restaurant then we will know that the snowball is rolling down hill big time.

Innovation is important to echoing green. Explain how your idea is truly innovative. Identify other organizations that are addressing this issue and how your approach is different and has the potential to be more effective.

Our idea is innovative because we are not just making organic, natural local food available we will be producing delicious, healthful, prepared "fast" food and selling it from outlets that reach the bulk of the population. Further we have a built-in model for replicating our approach, as our program incorporates training others to reproduce it to fit their own communities. Thus we are breaking through the socio-cultural-economic barriers and we are striking at the heart of the problem, the centralization of food production and distribution. Our approach to food production, do not follow recipes but learn an approach and techniques to produce meals out of what is currently local and affordable, is the novel lynchpin that can turn things around. Our central philosophy of training people to use local sources and thus de-centralize food production/distribution attacks the problem at the root. Other organizations are encouraging local food production through farmers markets and natural food stores, they are making inroads, but they leave the fast food market and all that goes with it untouched. We challenge that industry by competing directly with them for retail customers and for agricultural sources.

Building a new organization is challenging. How are you entrepreneurial? Describe your skills and experiences that demonstrate you can lead a start up organization.

Bill has started four different restaurants, all just about from scratch, all of which have been successful and drawn critical acclaim and a loyal customer base. Larry, relying on his Stanford Psychology PhD and Brooklyn street smarts, channeled his inner entrepreneur last spring.

Starting with zero resources in May 2009 and no foundation, government support, or major benefactor, he built upon Bill's skills to lead the creation of an organization that now has fifty-plus volunteers from every walk of life, established a home for it at a spectacular location beside the sea, organizes free weekly "soup events" with music that build community, landed a book contract to tell the story of the Common Good Soup Kitchen, and has the organization in the local press *every* week. Richard Grossinger, publisher of North Atlantic Books, social activist and author has written: "The Common Good Soup Kitchen brings together some remarkable people, including the two principles, chef and food expert Bill Morrison and retired psychology professor Larry Stettner. These men are both energetic, articulate, cutting edge and at a stage in their lives when they can devote themselves to the project."

Why are you uniquely qualified to lead your specific organization? Describe your experience working with this issue and population.

Bill is unique in being a Picasso of food. Just as one cannot appreciate Picasso without seeing his paintings, one cannot appreciate Bill's unique genius, nor the full potential impact of our project, without seeing and tasting his food. Larry is unique primarily for his people skills: his ability to communicate and his enthusiasm inspires people to join the effort and his ability to relate to them keeps them committed and working together. He was able to not only reach out to the economically disadvantaged of our community by drawing people from our local food voucher program to the free weekly soup events and distribution, but also involve many of them as volunteers as well, and in so doing unleashed some great talent. If we get to the third phase Bill will whip up some food for the interview and you will of course get to meet Larry head on and view his soup kitchen logo tattoo. To present some feel for the food, here are some of the fifty-two items that Bill created in ten days this past September for our café: poached squash and spinach puree, barley, corn and cashew salad, bulgur, carrot and mint salad, white bean and kale soup, eggplant and garlic soup, garlic and leek soup, wild rice salad with apricots and ginger.

How much money have you fund raised to date? What is your largest funder and what is the size of their grant? Provide an estimate of your total budget for each of the next two fiscal years.

We have raised close to $10,000 so far. The largest contributions are two $1,000 donations from individuals. Bill started "fund-raising" when people put money inside his soup kitchen mission statement book on a table in the hair salon in the center of town, then folks put donations on his kitchen table when they came by to pick up soup. When Larry came on board they held fund-raisers at churches, local cafes, the library and eventually their own café/soup kitchen space. The latter had brochures and the new comprehensive mission statement on tables, and walls hung with display boards detailing our program as well as food photos; we had free Wi-Fi and coffee, had all you can eat healthy breakfast bar and limited lunch menu. People put money in a bowl, in denominations of one to twenty dollars. That is where our money came from and continues to come from at present. We do have a 501(c)(3) fiscal sponsor and we will apply for our own federal tax-exempt status in 2010 when it gets cheaper and easier. Thanks to a supportive landlord, we estimate about 12K yearly to keep the soup program running as is, and 60K yearly to pre-launch the fast food operation as described above.

Why is co-leadership a superior model for your organization, compared to a single leader model?

Neither Bill nor Larry would have gotten past square one, nor could they get much further now, without the other. Larry would be totally lost without Bill's knowledge of food, not only preparation but suppliers, nutrition, etc. Bill would be totally lost without Larry's organizational and people skills. They not only complement each other, but they in fact inspire each other so that each in turn can do his thing and inspire others. Larry is in awe of what Bill can do with food and Bill is an awe of what Larry can do with organizing and inspiring people. A start-up takes incredible energy and they feed off of each other's energy. They conceived this together, they built it together, they will lead it to the next phase together. (Where would Sergei be without *his* Larry and vice-versa?) That being said they both visualize that after the next two years they themselves might become obsolete, except in a possible consulting role, as young people have already been drawn to this project, inspired to join the effort, young people that could well take on the leadership down the road.

How do you know each other? Describe the history of your relationship, including any shared work experiences and how you decided to create this organization together.

Bill and Larry met when Bill opened a small café in Southwest Harbor, Maine, near Larry's house. They began to play poker together, etc. Four years later, when Bill became executive chef at a new larger café in town, Larry became the musical booking agent for the café. Bill confided to Larry his natural food co-op dream one summer day. When he was laid off one winter day three years later, Bill, impressed with Larry's success in making Wednesday night winter nights a place of good cheer and light for the café and the entire little town, sought his advice about how to proceed with the co-op idea. About the same time, he started making soup and distributing it to local senior residences, to at least be able to cook and do some good for a short time. Then Bill heard an Obama speech and he read Paul Newman's book, *In Pursuit of the Common Good*. Bill was inspired to do more and began to make notes on his yellow pad. Larry read Newman's book, too. They began walking and talking in the woods, sharing the ideas that led to their realization that they had a common vision and complementary skills. They had their joint epiphany at the dinner meeting, produced a detailed mission statement and action plan, and the enthusiastic response to it launched the Common Good Soup Kitchen.

In a co-leadership model, titles help people understand what each partner does. What will your titles be? What will each of you do within the organization?

Larry's title will be director, visionary guru, chief disposer of trash, and scrubber of pots. Bill's will be executive chef and premier food honcho. Bill now consults on food production for soup events, scopes out local food sources, and cooks when he can. In the sparse local winter economy once more, he is forced to seek employment wherever he may find it. With support Bill can devote full time to take the project to the next level: creating food dishes, intensively scoping out and developing local food sources, producing food for and supervising the packaged prepared food distribution for sale to retail outlets. He will also be training new chefs and refining his training methods, and developing the detailed plans for the first Common Good Kitchen fast food franchise. Larry will seek out funding from every possible source, pay the bills, plan the finances, tirelessly promote the program in written and spoken word, plan fun events locally to continue to build community and publicize the CGK, hold volunteer meetings, form liaisons with other community kitchens in the region and seek out investors for that first fast food franchise.

What is the decision making process for your organization? When the two leaders have opposing views, how do you resolve the issue?

We have sit downs and walk-along meetings to talk things out. We try to work by consensus, turning things around in our minds and looking at different facets until we find what feels right for both of us. Often it is an "I like the idea overall, but what about this or that implication, not sure I like that, let's try to refine it" kind of discussion. If we disagree and have to make a decision rapidly, then Larry always defers to Bill in matters of food and Bill defers to Larry in matters of organization and personnel. Sometimes we agree to disagree, take a break and turn things over in our minds for a while longer and then come back later and try to reach consensus; if at impasse we may agree to consult our volunteers and/or advisory board. An important element is that we have our bedrock, our seven-page mission statement and action plan that we forged together in spring '09. It is our Bible, our constitution, our guide to our scope and our goals. So we never disagree on goals, only on the best means to get there. If all else fails we each get an armload of local, soft tomatoes, and throw them at each other from twenty yards apart; the one with the most blotches on him then defers to the other.

Summary of the Common Good Program
(April 1, 2010)

About the Common Good Soup Kitchen Community and Its Programs

The Common Good Soup Kitchen Community is an innovative community program that attempts to feed the body, mind and spirit of our community. We started in Feb 2009 when Chef Bill began delivering soups free of charge to the homes of those who could use such sustenance; we still do that but now have a home base where people can come together as well. Our spacious, inviting cafe is located at Seawall in SW Harbor, on Route 102 at 566 Seawall Road. It is adjacent to Acadia National Park and the Seawall Motel. It is perched on the rocky coast of Maine, overlooking the Atlantic Ocean.

Our primary mission is to nourish our community by bringing people together during the long and often economically difficult winter months. *We frankly are out to change what comes to mind when people hear the word soup kitchen:* at the Common Good it is a place for the whole community to gather, where the food, the view, the ambiance, the music, and the social occasion all come together in an appealing and nourishing way.

Our winter programs run from November thru April and include two community meal events each and every week. Our soup events take place on Fridays from noon to 2 p.m., and feature a great variety of soups as well as whole grain and green salads. Our Cabin Fever Family night suppers take place on Saturdays from 5:30 to 8:30. At both events truly delicious and nutritious food is served and there is *always live music* at both events. The Cabin Fever Saturday night events also feature balloon hats, make your own pizza for kids, and special entertainment and food items for the young ones as well as the great food and live music for all ages.

Everyone is welcome at all our events. There is never an admission fee or mandatory donation, but those who would like to contribute can through our donation bowl. Our events are true community events attended by people of all ages and all walks of life. The bulk of our support comes from donations garnered in the summer and the operation of the Common Good Café at Seawall from May through October; this gives us our nest egg for the winter. We are totally operated by volunteers and supported by grassroots donations. We have no government, foundation, or institutional affiliation or funding.

We endeavor to serve locally produced and harvested food products whenever possible and to keep our ingredients as natural as possible. Our food is produced by a cadre of volunteer chefs, who work with local farmers and fisherman in particular to be able to serve the finest food available locally in any given season. We always have a variety of both vegetarian and non-vegetarian options.

Too good to be true? Come on down to Seawall on Friday afternoon and/or Saturday night and see for yourself what we are all about! Information is at 207-266-2733; our email is commongoodsoup@gmail. com. You can also find our Web site by Googling *common good soup*. We always welcome new folks at our events and we can always use new volunteers who want to join the Common Good community of SW Harbor.

Appendix D
Additional Reading on Food

Web Sites

www.LocalHarvest.org
www.SustainableTable.org
www.WestonaPrice.org

Books

Cooksley, Valerie Gennari. *Seaweed: Nature's Secret to Balancing Your Metabolism, Fighting Disease, and Revitalizing Body and Soul.* New York: Stewart, Tabori & Chang, 2007

Holden, Chet. *Cooking for Fifty: The Complete Reference and Cookbook.* Hoboken: John Wiley & Sons, Inc., 2008.

Pollan, Michael. *In Defense of Food: An Eater's Manifesto.* New York: Penguin, 2009

Wrangham, Richard. *Catching Fire: How Cooking Made Us Human.* New York: Basic Books, 2009.

Wyler, Susan. *Cooking for a Crowd: Menus, Recipes and Strategies for Entertaining 10 to 50.* Emmaus: Rodale, Inc., 2005

Appendix E
Resource Materials for Organizing a Nonprofit

Web Sites

www.Echoinggreen.org
www.FoodCoop500.Coop

Books

Hotchner, A. E. and Paul Newman. *In Pursuit of the Common Good: Twenty-Five Years of Improving the World, One Bottle of Salad Dressing at a Time.* New York: Broadway, 2008.

Murray, Katherine and John Mutz. *Fundraising for Dummies.* San Francisco: John Wiley & Sons, Inc., 2010

Pyles, Loretta. *Progressive Community Organizing: A Critical Approach for a Globalizing World.* London: Routledge, 2009

Index

Salads

Soups

Stocks

Cooking Methods